Meet Ella

Meet Ella

The Dog Who Saved My Life

JAMES MIDDLETON

with FRANCES HARDY

PEGASUS BOOKS

NEW YORK LONDON

MEET ELLA

Pegasus Books, Ltd.
148 West 37th Street, 13th Floor
New York, NY 10018

ISBN: 978-1-63936-791-7

10 9 8 7 6 5 4 3 2 1

Printed in the United States of America
Distributed by Simon & Schuster
www.pegasusbooks.com

Pour Alizée, ma femme chérie.

For Inigo, you never met Ella, but she knew you
existed before we did.

And, of course, for Zulu, Inka, Luna, Mabel, Nala and Isla.

Contents

Prologue: My Darkest Night   1

1. No Creature Too Small   5
2. A Tiny Sightless Bundle   23
3. An Audience of Two Billion   39
4. Newborns, and a Calamity at Bucklebury   57
5. Ella's Royal Walkabout   75
6. My Descent into the Abyss   93
7. A Spark of Light in the Darkness   109
8. A Christmas Epiphany   131
9. Ella Plays Cupid   147
10. The Healing Power of Dogs   163
11. A Father's Blessing . . . and a Proposal   183
12. A Highland Loch-down . . . and a Home of Our Own   199
13. To Love and to Cherish   215
14. Pastures New   231
15. A Sadness Too Deep for Words   241
16. A Final Farewell . . . and New Beginnings   257
17. In Loving Memory   271

Acknowledgements   277

Prologue

My Darkest Night

———

All the colour has leached out of my life. I exist in a black and white world empty of emotion and feeling. I am perpetually agitated. If I go anywhere – to work, to a party, to the cinema – I feel compelled to leave. Yet once I do, I am still lost, aimless; pacing purposelessly.

There is no respite from this constant restlessness. It is almost impossible to describe the sense of unease. It is not so much a feeling as an absence of feelings. A void at my core. I have no purpose or direction. I cannot feel pleasure, excitement or anticipation.

There is a constant noise in my head like a radio that cannot be tuned; an unnerving crackle and buzz. The moment I find the delicate balance and the noise eases, the tiniest flinch of a muscle will set it off again. I cannot escape it.

I'm conflicted. I want to stay in bed all day, but my heart is racing so fast I feel it will burst out of my chest. As I lie there, it is as if someone is screaming into my face and the only way to stop them is to get up.

But there is nowhere to run when I do, no respite from the pounding of my heart, the assault on my senses.

Life is no longer worth living. I am suicidal. I contemplate ways of dying so I can get off the giddy roller-coaster that is sending me to the brink of madness.

I cannot sleep because my mind is in tumult. The insomnia is dizzying. I am utterly exhausted.

I feel misunderstood; a complete failure. I wouldn't wish the sense of worthlessness and desperation, the isolation and loneliness on my worst enemy. I think I'm going crazy.

Yet I know I am privileged; fortunate, too, to have a loving and close-knit family – Mum and Dad, my sisters Catherine and Pippa, their husbands William and James – but I push them all away. I do not answer their phone calls. Emails remain ignored. Invitations to visit go unheeded. I hide behind a double-locked door, unreachable.

One bleak November night in 2017, I reach my lowest ebb. It is around 2 a.m. and I cannot sleep. I've barely eaten for days, and when I do, the food clogs my throat and makes me retch. I pace round the flat where I live alone, the four walls that confine me seeming to close in on me. I feel suffocated, desperate for air.

I want to go outside but fear meeting late-night homecomers in the street.

At the top of the stairs there is a skylight. It leads to a flat roof where the water tanks sit. Once I went up there to fix a problem with the hot water. Since, during happier times, I have levered myself up through this opening in the roof and watched the sun set over a breathtaking London skyline, or climbed out to watch fireworks over the river.

Today I want to escape from myself. So I unhook the telescopic ladder, clamber up and propel myself onto the roof.

I stand and look out at London. There, spread out before me, is our majestic capital city – glittering lights, landmark buildings, the slow meander of the Thames – but now I do not see its glory.

I pace up and down, but there is no reprieve from the torment in my mind. Dark thoughts crowd in on me. What can I do to make them stop?

I think about jumping from the rooftop. Who would find me? A passing taxi driver? A neighbour?

I wonder, if I jump, could it possibly be construed as a tragic accident? That way my family, although they would grieve desperately, would be spared the added torture of knowing that I had ended my life by suicide.

As I pace, I look down through the skylight and see my spaniel Ella's gentle eyes looking back up at me. Like me, she has been wakeful all night. She senses my strange, agitated state of mind. She cannot climb the ladder – I would not want her to; it is too dangerous on the exposed rooftop and there are no safety rails – but she is standing at the foot of it imploring me with her eyes to come down.

I pace, look down again. My beloved Ella is still there. Do dogs ever feel despair, I wonder, or is it a peculiarly human malfunction of the mind? I imagine myself without her, and the chain of thought makes me pause.

What would Ella do without me? She depends on me and I on her. The feeling is entirely reciprocal.

I begin to pace again, back and forth for an hour or so, but find no comfort in the fresh air. The malaise I feel is so much worse than physical pain. It does not stop or even lessen. It silently warps the person I am. It is a corrosion of the mind.

I glance down the ladder again. Ella has not moved. Her brown eyes are still staring intently at me, soulful and pleading, and as my gaze locks on hers again, my brain quietens. In that instant I know I will not jump. What would happen to Ella if I died? How long would she wait alone in the flat for someone to find her?

I have loved her with every bit of my being since she was a tiny, sightless newborn pup. She has been my companion, my hope, my support through my darkest days. She has loved me unconditionally, faithfully. At night, when sleep eludes me, she is there on the bed beside me, willing me through the bleak pre-dawn hours.

Even when I have felt that the labour of living is not worth the effort, I've taken her for walks and fed her. She gives me purpose, a reason to be.

How can I contemplate leaving her now? What would she do without me?

Suddenly I realise that in the chill of the winter air I am shivering in my pyjamas. It is as if, for a second, reality has intruded. I haul myself back from the brink, slowly climb down the ladder and stroke Ella's silky head.

She is the reason I do not take that fatal leap. She is Ella, the dog who saved my life.

Chapter One

No Creature Too Small

I've always found animals more engaging companions than people. As a child, I used to put Tom, our family cat, in a wicker basket on my bike and cycle with him to the village shops.

I'd hatch eggs in the airing cupboard, cradling the tiny chicks tenderly in my hands, feeding them corn until they grew into a clutch of clucking hens.

My first pet, a hamster named Hammy, went with me everywhere in my pocket, constantly escaping and scuttling off behind the fridge or into the larder, until my long-suffering father got tired of launching rescue missions and implored me to keep him in his cage.

When Hammy died – my first, crushing taste of mortality – I begged for a replacement. Rushing home from a village fete where they were selling hamsters for fifty pence, I begged Mum for a pound so I could buy a pair, a brother and sister to be friends for each other.

I can still call to mind the cajoling tone I used. 'Please, please can I have them, Mum?' I had the cage and food already, I reasoned. So Mum relented. 'Yes, you can have them both,' she sighed with slight exasperation.

So I cycled back to the fete, breathless with excitement, and picked out the siblings, a girl and boy (or so I thought) who were to take the place of my departed hamster.

In fact, in my thrilled anticipation and excitement, I'd overlooked a couple of salient points: the 'hamsters', it emerged, were in fact guinea pigs; and they were both males. Max and Harry, I called them.

But my endlessly patient parents accepted our unexpected rodent adoptees. We procured a bigger hutch for them and they settled in comfortably at Bucklebury, our family home in Berkshire. Then, when I was seven, we upgraded once again and they were joined by rabbit Jess.

Jess and I forged a bond of trust. I taught her to sit and stay; she learned to recognise her name and respond to it. She even hopped to heel on a lead, bounding along beside me as I walked to the shops. I rewarded her with a carrot for these extraordinary feats of obedience. These early pets instilled a mutual understanding. Actually, I grew to love them, and my compassion extended to the entire animal kingdom.

A dying mouse floundering in the school swimming pool? I'd dive in to retrieve it. If a bird broke a wing, I'd nurture it, warm it in the airing cupboard, feed it by pipette, ferry it to the RSPCA. No cause, however desperate, was abandoned; no ailing creature was too much trouble.

In fact, at my prep school, St Andrew's in Pangbourne, it became my mission to rescue any creature in distress: beetles struggling upside down on pathways were gently set on their feet again; and spiders retrieved from bathtubs were liberated into woodpiles, where they could forage happily for grubs and flies.

I'm sure now that my teachers must have been exasperated by my philanthropic rescue missions, especially when protracted negotiations with animal charities were involved. How many hypothermic mice could the RSPCA accommodate? How many dying blackbirds? Needless to say, I was on first-name terms with all the inspectors.

My sisters, Catherine and Pippa, are, respectively, five and three years older than me. Growing up surrounded by three strong, capable women felt like having three mothers, and I would rely on Catherine and Pippa for advice.

They never dismissed me as their little squirt of a brother who wasn't worthy of their attention. On the contrary, they let me join in their games and included me in their friendships – they still do to this day. While we were at prep school together, they would fuss over me like mother hens, reporting back to our parents on my many (mild) misdemeanours, more in a spirit of concern than because they were telltales.

Never noted for my neat appearance, I'd emerge from some ramble with a borrowed dog, my shirt untucked, my hands smeared with mud and brambles snagged in my hair, to be reprimanded and given a bad order mark, which would be chalked up on a board. These accumulated and were only redressed by good order marks. Naturally, Catherine and Pippa, being exemplary students, managed to get through their entire school life without a single demerit, but I amassed a handful of them every term.

The system worked like this: since bad order marks were cancelled out by good order marks, it seemed that every commendation my sisters notched up would be nullified by one of my wrongdoings.

So while the female Middletons would be applauded for being helpful to teachers – opening doors and carrying books for them – I'd undo all their kind deeds by scampering along the corridor instead of walking because I was late for a lesson. (Two bad order marks for the price of one there.) And while Catherine and Pippa got full marks for spelling tests and top grades for essay-writing, I lagged behind on both counts, accruing a batch of misconduct marks for my below-par school work.

The net result of this was that at the end of each term when the marks – favourable and negative – for each house were added up, the Middleton family did not actually make an impact either way.

My school reports charted my academic shortcomings, but there was always a wry aside, a gentle allusion to my affinity with the animal kingdom. 'If only James could apply himself as much to his school studies as to his humanitarian work with animals,' my teachers would sigh via their pens.

The thing is, I wasn't wilfully undisciplined, just mischievous. One teacher, Mr Outram, had a golden retriever; another, Mr Embury, a poodle. I'd clamour to take both dogs for walks and thought that I'd be given credit for my sense of responsibility and helpfulness.

The trouble was, I was always late back for lessons, having become so immersed in my adventures with the dogs in the woods near our school that I just forgot about returning from break.

I'd hear the bell ring and scamper back breathless, bedraggled dog in tow, ready to face the inevitable bad order mark. Even so, the teachers felt I was trustworthy enough to take their dogs out again, and this built my confidence.

This confidence clearly shone through, and in my final year I was awarded the Headmaster's Prize, an accolade, on this occasion, given to a good-natured boy who would never breeze effortlessly into university with a clutch of glittering exam results, but would rather perish himself than abandon a dying animal.

Academically, I lagged behind woefully, so I was desperate to counter this shortcoming by being considered responsible. Because the truth was that until I could prove myself I would never have the dog of my own that I yearned for.

Until I could get a dog every other pet was a stand-in. But I made the most of the animals I was entrusted with. And I continued to hone my skills as a potential dog-trainer on my rabbit.

Sometimes I thought I'd be happier as an animal. Mum tells me that when I was four years old, I even crouched down to eat the cat's food from his bowl on the floor. (I got a severe telling-off for that.)

I pleaded with Mum and Dad for a dog. They resisted, but I did my best to make myself indispensable to other dog-owners, offering myself for walking duty whenever I was needed.

I befriended every dog in the village. When our neighbours moved away, taking their Rottweiler – a vast, slavering beast I'd fearlessly wrestle with in their kitchen – I was inconsolable. Until, that is, new neighbours moved in with a couple of lovable black Labs who became my new playmates.

I adored my grandparents' British bulldog, Gibson, and would rush to their house, barely pausing to acknowledge the old folk before scampering off with the dog on a kite-flying expedition or fishing trip.

My first dawning awareness that a dog could become a loyal companion – actually an extension of myself – was when I read the *Famous Five* books. I warmed to George and her mongrel Timmy, a dog so devoted, clever and affectionate that their bond became inviolable.

In this make-believe world, a dog could accompany a child to boarding school. In my real world this would never happen, but I could wish and hope for the next best thing.

Being a few years younger than my sisters, I was still at prep school when they graduated to Marlborough College. And every time I was dragged along to spectate at one of their sports matches, I'd sidle off and beg the headmaster's wife to let me take her beautifully groomed Old English Sheepdog for an amble round the grounds.

These innocuous-sounding walks escalated into *Famous Five*-style adventures (although in our case we were an intrepid duo). At the final whistle, as my sisters emerged triumphant or deflated from their sporting feats, a bedraggled, mud-flecked vision – half human, half canine – materialised from a nearby copse, having splashed heedlessly through puddles and streams for the past hour.

I still remember the look of amused exasperation on the face of the headmaster's wife. 'Oh James,' she'd sigh, retrieving her prize dog. 'I think you'll both need a bath after this.'

By now, my longing for a dog of my own had become an ache of yearning. I craved a companion in my adventures. A solace at times of sadness. Actually a friend who loved me unconditionally – without judgement or ridicule. Because I was an unusual boy. Try as I might, I could not get enthused by football – either spectating or playing – and would rather tinker around with a tractor than kick a ball.

My principal passion, from my earliest boyhood and through adolescence, continued to be animals. Had I not been dyslexic, and my mind a constantly bubbling cauldron of restless energy that made concentration on schoolwork almost impossible, I'd have loved to have become a vet. But I knew I'd never make the grade academically.

It is ironic, really, that my parents finally gave in to my incessant pleas for a dog when I was 13 and just going off to boarding school. To my unending delight, Tilly, a golden retriever puppy, arrived, and although she was a family dog, it is no surprise that I appropriated her as my own. This boisterous little bundle of wet-nosed energy was all I had ever yearned and wished for. Yet she was arriving just as I was leaving home.

As I stroked her silky golden head and said my tearful goodbyes when I left for my first day at Marlborough College, I was choked with sadness. Consumed by homesickness at school – the yearning manifested itself as a physical pain like an ache in the heart – I willed away the seconds until the weekend, when I'd be back at Bucklebury and Tilly would bound into my outstretched arms.

I felt at sea in those early days at boarding school. I missed the easy familiarity of the tight-knit bunch of friends I'd made at prep school; the fact that they accommodated and understood my eccentricities, my obsessive love of animals, my indifference to football scores.

What was more, I was starting from scratch at Marlborough. Nobody knew about, or made allowances for, the quirks of the slightly scrawny Middleton Minor, who had arrived in the wake of his two accomplished big sisters.

It was assumed that I would be as talented as they were at sports, and I was automatically put into the first team for rugby, but in my debut match I got so spectacularly pummelled I was instantly relegated to a much lower division. Comments like 'Are you *really* a Middleton?' echoed round the changing room and pitches. They cut to my heart, and my confidence – buoyant at prep school – waned in this less forgiving new environment.

Sensitive and vulnerable, I was an easy target for teasing and mockery. There is a fine line between good-humoured practical jokes and bullying, and I don't want to cast myself as a victim, but I think some of the boys set out to intimidate me.

In the vast dining hall at Marlborough, we had to take our trays – laden with cutlery, crockery and water glass – back to a rotating conveyor belt once we had finished our meal. Occasionally the unwary would trip and the contents of their trays would go flying, the crash as the plates, dishes, knives and forks hit the floor reverberating in the cavernous room.

One lunchtime, as I was returning my tray, an older boy stuck his foot out on purpose and I sailed headlong over it, smack onto the floor, my tray soaring skywards then descending, its contents smashing with a deafening clatter. As it did so, the hall erupted in sarcastic applause and every head turned to see who the klutz was.

Blushing furiously, I scraped up the debris and scuttled off, humiliated as my tormentor had intended. I knew the boy. He had wanted to date Pippa but she had refused him. This was his way of retaliating. There was one consolation: I knew she'd made the right decision and would be better off without him.

I wonder if my oversized wool blazer also made me a target. I was a slight boy, dwarfed by a garment several sizes too big – Mum had bought it so I would 'grow into it'; in fact it saw me through until sixth form, by which time it was as tight as a sausage skin – and one morning I was sitting in chapel enveloped in this substantial garment.

The service progressed and we got to prayers. As I sat in the pew, my head bowed in silent contemplation, the quiet was pierced by a sudden strident and insistent beeping.

It didn't take long to realise where the noise was coming from: the pocket of my own blazer. A prankster had put an alarm clock in it, and, knowing the exact moment silent prayers would begin, had set it to go off in the middle of them. To make matters worse, he had pinned up the pocket's opening so I struggled to retrieve the clock and stop the alarm.

The horror of it all consumed me. The chaplain's appalled gaze met my beseeching one. Every head in chapel swivelled to stare at me.

It wasn't my fault, of course, but I was compelled to take the punishment: a pink chit – the reprimand for the worst kind of offence – was issued and I had to run a mile at 7 a.m. to the Wedgwood Stone, so called because it commemorated Allen Wedgwood, who was killed at Gallipoli in 1915.

Actually, this penalty wasn't a burden to me at all. I enjoyed the early-morning run in the fresh air. In later years, I built friendships by accompanying pupils who had been issued with pink chits on their dawn jogs to the monument, just for the fun of it. In fact, it helped shape the resilient person I am today.

But in those early years, when I was still finding my feet, I was often unhappy, and my solace – in Tilly's absence – was walks with my housemaster's dogs, brown Labrador Maddie, and Owen, a Border collie. Whenever I had a spare hour, I'd tap on his kitchen window and beg to take them out, my companions in fantastical imaginary adventures that I'd conjure up in my inventive mind.

The dogs grew to like me, and they followed me around. When I was compelled, reluctantly, to join in a game of five-a-side football, Maddie would bound up to me in the middle of the pitch, a stick clamped hopefully in her mouth, and stay there, ignoring the other boys' jeers, waiting for me to throw it for her.

I'd break off from playing to hurl the stick, which never made me popular with my teammates, who were intent on winning, not appeasing friendly dogs. And there were school rules I'd flagrantly infringe, encouraging Owen to follow me into the boarding house – hoping, even, that he wouldn't be missed if he curled up at the foot of my bed for the night. But of course he was, and we'd both get a sharp reprimand.

It was 2001, the end of my first-year Christmas holidays, and we'd gone out to get my hair cut and buy trainers for the new term, when I broke my ankle – unglamorously, by falling off a raised pavement in a multistorey car park.

Mum and Pippa were waiting in the car for me while I paid for the parking at Mum's request. I ran across to the meter, misjudged the height of the kerb, rolled over on my ankle and came hobbling back to the car.

Neither Mum nor my sister were very charitable when I complained constantly about how much it hurt – until, that is, I got home and took off my sock to reveal a livid bruise spreading across my entire foot. After driving me to hospital that evening, poor Mum burst into tears when the X-ray revealed a broken bone.

'I'm so sorry I wasn't sympathetic,' she said, fretting about how challenging it would be for me navigating school on my crutches. Actually, it was even more of an ordeal than she'd feared, because the crutches were stolen by a fellow pupil, so I had to hop around until a teacher intervened and retrieved them for me.

Life, I realised with adolescent resignation, wasn't fair, but I did learn compassion and sensitivity, and I stood up to the bullies who picked on other boys.

Our school encouraged us to be intrepid. There have been many adventurous Malburians: Frank Bickerton, an alumnus from the turn of the twentieth century, was an Arctic explorer, treasure-hunter, soldier, aeronaut, entrepreneur and film-maker.

Then there was Dr David Pratt, whose invaluable contribution to the trans-Antarctic expedition in 1955 earned him a Polar Medal. Closer to my time were explorer and writer Redmond O'Hanlon from the sixties, and mountaineer Jake Meyer, the youngest Briton to climb Mount Everest.

I wouldn't presume to align myself with any of these esteemed figures, but I will say that I can add escapologist, handyman and nocturnal explorer to the dubious list of accomplishments I acquired at school.

During a design technology lesson, I liberated a screwdriver, and later used it to unscrew the safety locks on the windows of our dormitory. Then, I hit upon an idea: I'd make a rope ladder.

I hit on an audacious – and slightly dodgy – scheme for acquiring the necessary materials from the design technology storeroom. I was making a collapsible garden parasol (an entirely legitimate project for an exam) with lots of pulleys and ropes, and I requested slightly more rope than needed so I could use the surplus for my ladder.

Having smuggled the excess rope out of the workshop in my rucksack, I got to work knotting and tying so it would comfortably bear the weight of an adolescent boy.

My plan was to let it unfurl out of the open window at night, so everyone in the dormitory – except the person picked to stay and be lookout – could go night-walking.

We managed this quite successfully without detection for several weeks, I alone being able to appease Maddie and Owen, hushing them when they barked as we made our escape.

I'm sorry to say we didn't get up to anything nefarious on these nocturnal walks – we just trekked through woods and fields under cover of darkness, and that was thrill enough – but inevitably one night we were discovered. Our lookout called us in a panic to say there was a bed check, so we all raced back, scaled the rope ladder and threw ourselves into bed before the teacher arrived to do his rounds.

But in our scurrying haste to climb back through the window, the last boy forgot to pull up the rope ladder, and next morning it caught the eye of a passing teacher.

'Where did this ladder come from?' he asked us.

'Well, I made it, sir,' I admitted, volunteering no more than the necessary information.

I was suspended for a few days, but actually there was no punishment: Mum and Dad had gone on holiday and I couldn't be sent home.

Now, as an adult, I recognise the amiable, mischievous rogue I was, always straining to break free from the classrooms that I felt imprisoned me.

I hated being confined by four walls. Study was anathema to me and the written word baffling; even disquieting. Words jumped and blurred on the page. When it was my turn to read aloud in class, my efforts bore no resemblance to the sentences printed in front of me. I remember the laughter that rippled round the room as I misread words and stumbled over pronunciations before, capitulating to my inability to decode the letters, literally inventing a story.

I was an outcast. And although I kept track of football scores and forced myself to learn the names of managers and players, I was afraid to join in with the easy patter of my classmates, fearing they would sniff out my try-hard approach and jeer at my stupidity.

My interests set me apart, too. While most boys plastered their walls with posters of football teams or bikini-clad girls, mine were festooned with pictures of Land Rovers and engines. I squirrelled away old car parts and cycled to the local garage to watch intently as the mechanic tinkered with greasy machinery.

These obsessions alienated me from my classmates. But dogs never judged me. Mum asked repeatedly if I wanted to bring friends home to stay at weekends. But truthfully all I wanted to do was to see Tilly.

When she drove to fetch me from school on those Fridays when we were allowed to come home, she would be full of questions about how my week had gone, but I ignored them and asked instead about our dog. What had she been doing? Had she missed me? I'd jump into the boot of the hatchback with Tilly and travel alongside her, chatting to her all the way home.

Throughout my teens, my two obsessions, with dogs and all things mechanical, flourish. Weeks before I am due to turn 18, in the spring of 2005, my father asks what I'd like for my birthday. He gives me a choice: a little second-hand Peugeot 206 or a dilapidated and ancient tractor. A tractor? Yes, he knows in his heart that I'll choose the quirky option – and I do.

So he drives me down to Devon. It's a proper father-and-son road trip and we set off at the crack of dawn to find the farm where the venerable old vehicle has been advertised for sale.

When we get there, its owner, a strong, sturdy-looking chap, is practically in tears. He is loath to part with his rusty old tractor and explains that he's had it from new. The sheaf of paperwork he hands us documents its entire service history. It still has its original number plate. And although it's in urgent need of a lick of paint, it starts on the button. The engine has a lovely purr to it.

Dad and I load it onto the trailer. As we drive back to Berkshire through lanes bright with wild flowers, I reflect on how thrilled I am with my gift. Catherine and Pippa received beautiful jewellery when they turned 18. I have a tractor, and I decide to honour her by naming her Tilly, after our beloved dog.

The restoration of Tilly becomes a project – and naturally her namesake, golden retriever Tilly, is my ever-present companion in this. I build her a little platform where she can sit safely, and we chug to the shops, Tilly comfortably ensconced on her perch, eliciting the amused interest of pedestrians as we pass by.

Tilly is a sweet-natured dog, loyal and obliging. She shepherds me from boyhood through adolescence and on to the cusp of adulthood. When I'm making my first tentative foray into dating, she's there, dispelling awkward silences – she has a talent for appearing with a tennis ball when there is a lull in the conversation – and giving me an excuse to go for walks in the countryside, hold hands, sneak a first kiss.

But she is very much a Middleton family dog. And, truthfully, what I want more than anything is a dog of my own.

Meanwhile, I do so badly in my final school exams – including setting a humiliating school record of failing chemistry A-level four times – that my poor mum is reduced to tears. Dad says my expensive education has been 'a waste of money'.

I take a gap year, but mine is not crammed with travel and horizon-expanding adventures as other pupils' are. As they set off to trek through Costa Rica or the Antarctic, or to volunteer in the Peruvian Andes or remote African villages, I spend six months in a sixth-form college in London labouring through my A-level retakes.

The one spark of light in this dark time of dusty classrooms, of swatting and cramming – I've sat retakes so frequently I can practically recite the syllabus by heart – is Tilly.

She loves to come with me on the old Routemaster bus, hopping onto the open end and standing there with me, proffering her paw as passengers get on and off. It is one of her endearing qualities: she rests her paw on your hand as if she is shaking it.

People give her treats. If they balance them on her nose, at the command she flicks them up in the air then catches them in her mouth. It's her party trick. She gets an awful lot of treats.

We try the Underground too, but it's a challenge to carry her up and down the escalators – she's a big, heavy dog – so we revert to the bus or seek out Tube stations with stairs so she can be my classroom companion at college.

We students are a motley assortment, with some, like me, taking resits and others who have been expelled from school, so our teacher is grateful that we turn up at all and indulges the presence of a dog.

I realise how firmly Tilly is embedded in my affections on the day she goes missing at Bucklebury. It is Bonfire Night and she is scared of fireworks. We go to a display in our village, leaving her at home but forgetting the ground-floor window left slightly ajar.

When we return, she has disappeared. My heart gives a lurch of fear. I drive round all night, stopping, searching with a torch, calling her name. A sense of panic and loss consumes me. All sorts of thoughts flash through my mind: what if she has been taken, or hit by a car? The sick feeling in my stomach does not disperse.

But when I get home, exhausted, distraught, in the early hours, there is Tilly. Someone has returned her. She rushes to me, still shaking with nerves. I am shaking too. 'I will never let you out of my sight again,' I tell her, burying my face in her fur.

This sense that we could have lost her through a moment of careless inattention sharpens my sense of responsibility: when I have my own dog, I will cherish it as a parent does a child.

Then, as summer draws to a close, to our delight Tilly is pregnant. I am to have one of her pups. It has been promised; I cannot suppress the smile that springs to my lips whenever I think about it. There are two causes for celebration, because I also finally scrape into Edinburgh University – by the skin of my teeth with the minimum permitted grades.

Then comes a crushing blow. Tilly loses her litter. Three pups are stillborn and the fourth is so weak and tiny he does not live. The weight of sadness – for Tilly and for myself, deprived of the puppy I yearned for – casts its shadow as I drive myself to Scotland, but already the thought is forming: I will look for another puppy. I'll finally get my longed-for dog.

I'm in my sisters' hand-me-down car and it's crammed with the paraphernalia of student life: duvet, speakers, mugs and crockery, battered holdalls. Before I've even got to my room, my best friend from school, Nick, spots me and rushes over laughing. 'So you got here in the end. How did you manage that?' He can't actually believe I've made the grade.

For the next term, I make occasional forays to lectures, but I'm easily distracted. I'll stop for a coffee in a bookshop and idle away hours scribbling ideas for businesses in my notebook (like Mum and Dad, who started their company, Party Pieces, from their kitchen, I am by nature an entrepreneur), realising with a sudden jolt that I've missed the lecture entirely.

I miss Tilly so much that occasionally I drive home to collect her for a stay in Scotland, smuggling her through the entrance to my student halls in the dark or waiting until the kinder security guards are on duty and begging them to turn a blind eye to my visitor.

But it isn't fair to my parents to appropriate the family dog on a whim, and I'm certain – against precedent and rules – that I'll be able to look after my own puppy at university. It's just a question of finding exactly the right one.

– 22 –

Chapter Two

A Tiny Sightless Bundle

———

It is hardly a revelation to me that I'm unsuited to academic study, but my parents – convinced that a degree is the only option for me – have yet to be persuaded that my destiny lies elsewhere.

But for all my reservations, I shall be eternally thankful for the time I spend in Edinburgh, because it is thanks to Ben, a university friend, that I find my adored dog Ella.

Ben's brother Luke lives on Islay, the southernmost island of the Inner Hebrides, and there are many Friday evenings when we'll drive to catch the ferry to his home on this beautiful and remote outpost.

There I meet Luke's black cocker spaniel Zulu, a dog of such character and mischief that he instantly charms me. Zulu has all the acting talents of a seasoned thespian. If he wants to get your attention, he'll pretend to have hurt his foot and adopt a convincing hobble. Then, the minute your back is turned, he'll race off, his foot miraculously restored.

I've never met working cocker spaniels before, and on these trips, in the company of Zulu, I conclude that they're exactly the breed for me. Easy-going, affectionate and fizzing with restless energy, they're also a suitable size to fit under your arm if you need to carry them. And they crave the attention I'm longing to give.

Needless to say, if Luke and his wife want to go away for the weekend, I'm first in the queue to dog-sit.

'If Zulu ever sires puppies, I'd love one of them,' I tell them. Actually, they say, the deed has already been done – with Mabel, a lemon-coloured cocker spaniel. By happy coincidence, Mabel belongs to the parents of one of Pippa's friends.

My sister was also at Edinburgh University, so such chance collisions of our worlds aren't rare, but in this case I feel I am destined to have one of Mabel's pups.

But I have to prove myself worthy of one: a responsible, loving and committed person, a lifelong companion for a dog. I make the first tentative phone call.

'Hi, I'm James, Pippa Middleton's brother. I hear you have a litter of puppies. I'd be really interested in one.'

On paper I don't look good. I'm a student – well, for the time being at least – and surely the point about being a student, all reasonable logic would dictate, is that you're free to stay out late any time you want, take off on a whim, keep unsocial hours. Not an auspicious start when it comes to providing the stability and routine a dog needs. But I am prepared – glad, actually – to forfeit all those freedoms to become a dog parent.

Mabel's owners agree to let me meet the litter, so I drive to the Borders to visit them. Mabel greets me at the door, as excited to show off her pups as I am to see them. I'm set on a girl – it would be wonderful to breed from her one day – and there she is. Ella.

The name fits. It has been circling in my mind for months, like an incantation. I like its brevity and the lilting 'a' at the end; I can imagine calling it to her, and it suits her just fine.

I hold her, this tiny, wriggling, sightless bundle, and suddenly everything makes sense. She is the one for me. Call it instinct, if you like, but this vulnerable little bundle of jet-black fur entrances me. From the second I hold her, I am in love.

I think about the warnings that a dog will restrict my life. I know, incontrovertibly, that the opposite is true. She will signal a breaking-free, the start of a new life in which I'm liberated to be myself.

But it is not sealed yet. I am still being interviewed; my strength of purpose tested. Ella is too young to leave her mother. Will I come back in a few weeks to see her again? Of course I will.

Three weeks later, I go back. Ella's character traits are starting to emerge. Her siblings lie cuddled together on the floor. She wanders off, intrepid, alone. I pick her up, stroke her, and she falls asleep in my arms.

I remember a cup of tea waiting for me on the table. I daren't reach out for it in case I disturb her. The merest twitch of a muscle might wake her. I let her sleep on, pleased that she is content, at ease with me.

Then, when she awakens and patters off, I get down to her level with my head on the floor and let her walk around and sniff me. She seems to like me. Maybe it is one of those intuitive connections, inviolable as a lifelong friendship. When you've met your match, you know it, just as you know the person you will marry, I imagine.

I don't want to exhaust her, to swamp her with affection, so it is decided: I will come back in four weeks to collect her. Ella will be mine. And I will make a promise always to take care of her, just as she – I know – will take care of me.

Ella is eight weeks old – still tiny, but by now weaned and vaccinated – when she is ready to leave the pack. I've kitted myself out with all the paraphernalia I need to welcome a new puppy into my life – a crate, a bed, bowls – and I set off to bring her home.

The sense of excitement on this new-minted day grows as I drive closer to her. I arrive to a briefing about how to care for her, and I make a vow that she will be well disciplined and mannerly; a dog who will endear herself to all. She will not beg for food or jump up or run off. She will return when I call her name and walk to heel. Above all, she will be with me wherever I go. These are the silent pledges I make.

As she curls up in her crate for the journey to Berkshire, beside me on the passenger seat, and I comfort her with glances and soft words, the sudden realisation that she is alone – separated from her siblings – seems to strike her, and her squeals are heartbreaking.

So we stop and I reassure her, nuzzle her face, stroke her, and she settles. By the time we get to Bucklebury, her old excitement has returned.

Mum and Dad have gone on holiday and Catherine and William are staying at our family home. William has now become a fixture in our lives, established as Catherine's boyfriend, a welcome member of the clan. I have not told him or Catherine about Ella. They know I am getting a puppy, but they don't realise her arrival is imminent.

So I let Ella announce herself I place her on the doorstep and allow her to make her entrance into her new family home.

From the off, she is a confident little soul. She bounds so excitedly over the threshold that dear Tilly yelps and runs off in the opposite direction, coming to a sliding stop on the wooden floor and lying under the stairs, sulking. Later she looks at me quizzically as if to ask, 'Is this brash new intruder actually going to stay?'

Then Ella bounds into the kitchen to introduce herself to Catherine and William.

'I thought you sounded a bit sheepish about something when you phoned,' smiles William.

'But whose is she?' puts in Catherine.

'She's mine.'

'You're not serious. Do Mum and Dad know?'

'Er . . . no.'

'So how are you going to tell them?'

'I haven't got that far yet.'

There is laughter; I think even longing from them to have a dog of their own one day.

Tilly needs to assert her superiority. She is, of course, top dog in our household, the matriarch, with privileges that are conferred with age. She wants to ensure that the interloper does not overstep the mark.

At mealtimes Tilly is permitted to sit near the table – she is, of course, a well-mannered dog and never begs for titbits – while Ella has to stay in her crate. And for a while Tilly's wariness of this boisterous little newcomer persists.

But it doesn't take long for the dogs to grow to love each other. Ella is inherently amiable, reliable, kind – but of course she's much more than that. She's a dog who touches the hearts of all who know her, a dog of such acute intelligence that she intuits mood and, I believe, understands people's feelings.

But with a new puppy come responsibilities on both sides: learning and training are two-way streets. When Ella howls at 3 a.m., I go to the door, speak calmly to her through it, but do not go in. She must learn to be reassured by my voice but not to expect me to pet her when she wakes in the early hours.

When she is excited or overwhelmed, she pees on the carpets. I am constantly scrubbing them. She chews the legs of the kitchen chairs, her little teeth marks imprinted in the wood.

In those early days, routine and discipline are my watchwords. I am strict while she is learning. She can have more freedom later. Recall is the first vital lesson. When I call her name, she must learn to come to me immediately. I drill this lesson by hiding behind a tree if she does not respond at once. In her slight panic at my disappearance, the lesson is instilled. She understands she must return to my side at the first call of 'Ella'.

Once she has learned these rudiments and we're bonded by mutual trust, we can begin our adventures together. And what wonders are in store!

But first there is the small matter of telling Mum and Dad about the new member of the household. I figure that the best time to do it is while they're still on holiday. If their response is unfavourable, the phone signal can suddenly become a problem.

I call them in the Caribbean. We talk about university. I'm taking resits, having failed my first year. My parents are intent on me staying the course. In my mind I have already left, but I leave the door open a crack.

The conversation falters. Ella, hungry, sets up an insistent yapping.

'What's that?' asks Mum.

'James has got a dog,' shouts Catherine above Ella's barking.

'What? Are you serious?' (We've been here before. I can imagine the incredulous eye-rolling.)

'But just wait till you see her. You'll love her,' I insist, before adding without much conviction – or truthfulness – 'There are lots of students with dogs. I'll make it work.'

What no one but me knows at this point is that my tenure as a student has a very short lease to run. Although I set off back to Edinburgh in January with Ella in tow, I know I will not be staying the course.

It is – despite my protestations to the contrary – very unusual for a student to own a dog. But when I arrive back in Edinburgh, Ella settles, for the time being at least, into university life, living in our chaotic student flat, shared with three of my friends.

I quickly discover that she is an asset when it comes to endearing me to potential dates. 'I've got to go home now to let my dog out,' I announce on nights out, and quite often I find it is a winning chat-up line. What young woman can resist a man who rushes home from nightclubs to look after his puppy?

Sometimes I stay out too late and Ella reprimands me in her own way, once even peeing on my pillow to chastise me for failing to get back in time. If she is really cross, she doesn't greet me at the door but sulks inside until I rush to her, ruffle her fur and apologise.

Then she is appeased and nuzzles me to signal her forgiveness.

We go on walks together, twice a day, over the cobbled streets. Twice a week we scamper up Arthur's Seat and look down on the vista of the handsome city unfurling beneath us.

Ella comes with me when I play rugby and watches from the sidelines. When we wander home via the pub, she is indulged by the bar staff with her favourite tipple of cold tea.

I remember fondly the time we stop to eat mussels in a pub. Ella has her own portion – steamed without garlic and sauce – and eats them with relish.

One day, loath to leave her even for a couple of hours, I smuggle her into the lecture hall and she sits obediently and unobtrusively at my feet. She seems to know she must be discreet – that she's not really permitted to be there – and it is only when other students keep bobbing below the desk to stroke her velvety head that the lecturer's suspicions are aroused.

He glances towards me, curiosity piqued. Why are half the class distracted by something that's happening at my feet? He strides up, irritated, to take a look and is not placated by Ella's beseeching brown eyes.

He evicts us both and tells me not to bring her back – which neither endears him to me nor encourages me to complete my degree.

I'm once again at sea academically, floundering through my essay-writing, freighted by the burden of my dyslexia, taking longer to complete every assignment than my peers and failing to enjoy any aspect of my studies.

I settle on three disparate courses – criminology, environmental sciences and geography – for the simple reason that I'm pretty certain they will all be multiple choice. I take a thick felt pen into the first exam so I can tick the relevant boxes, horrified to find that I have to write a three-part essay. My offering is a mass of incoherent splodges and disconnected sentences. In my mind I've already surrendered.

University is not for me, I tell my distraught parents. Mum cries again. Dad is starting to despair of me. But I stick to my guns and – although I don't yet announce the fact to Mum and Dad – decide to quit.

My mind is a bubbling cauldron of ideas and I decide to set up my own cake kit company. Mum and Dad have their online business selling banners, balloons, tableware; everything you'd want for a child's party – except the cake. And every party needs a cake, doesn't it?

I've identified a gap in the market and I'm hoping that, armed with my business plan and my self-taught expertise as a baker, my parents will want to team up with me. I'm already framing the sales pitch in my mind: cakes for every occasion with the ingredients weighed out, measured and dispatched to hard-pressed parents who can then read the easy-to-follow recipes and produce their own party confections.

As I bide my time before leaving university altogether, my student flat in Edinburgh becomes the testing centre for these creations. I bake princess fairy castles using empty loo rolls as the templates for towers and ice cream cones for their turrets.

I produce pirates' chests full of chocolate coins wrapped in gold foil. Edible dinosaurs lumber across the kitchen table with cochineal-coloured scales. The kitchen surfaces are permanently dusted with icing sugar. Sprinkles festoon the counters. It is like some kind of mad Willy Wonka's cake factory.

Ella watches as I whisk eggs and fold in flour. She sits patiently under the table waiting for scraps of cake mix to drop, then dispatches them furtively. She learns a party trick: I discover that her mouth is so gentle she can carry an egg in it without even cracking it.

My flatmates return from nights out to test the cakes. I task them with following the recipes too, thinking that if they can do it when they're drunk or hung-over, a burned-out parent will find them child's play.

When not experimenting in the kitchen, Ella and I go off on adventures. We often visit Luke on Islay at weekends, and a few times we miss the last ferry to the island and have to wait overnight for the one at 6 a.m. We curl up to sleep together in the back of the car, gazing at a wide sky sprinkled with stars.

We camp out, too, on Islay's beaches. I improvise a tent from a tarpaulin and driftwood, then light a fire to heat boulders so we have our own home-made sauna.

These wild adventures, grown-up versions of my *Famous Five*-style schoolboy escapades with borrowed dogs, are the ones we love.

I don't consider Ella my pet; she is my equal, and while I don't humanise her, I respect her needs, the most pressing of which is to be with me.

So wherever I go, she goes too.

If I'm paddleboarding, she sits on a grip mat on the front of the board. When we go to the Lake District – a place I've loved since boyhood – we paddle out to an island on Lake Windermere.

We go for a walk and a dip. Ella loves swimming; she also learns that she must time her swim carefully. If she waits until the end of the walk, she'll need to dry off in an outhouse or shed when we get home. If she has a dip at the start, she'll have time to breeze-dry her coat.

So sophisticated is her understanding that I begin to think she is an extension of me; our unspoken bond is such that she even knows when I'm thinking of having a swim and patters down to the rock pool or river just as the idea is forming in my mind.

She loves the snow, too, and we go skiing together in the Swiss Alps. I do not follow the crowds ascending on ski lifts but plot a route off-piste. Ella follows in my tracks as I ski along remote Alpine paths, away from the hordes in the resorts. We watch marmots, deer and snow hares from a quiet distance. Ella does not chase them. She has been schooled to stay close, but her questing nose is sniffing the air long before I have spotted a herd of deer.

Then when I've skied back down the mountain, I pick her up and cradle her carefully, as I would a child, and she almost falls asleep in my arms.

She is my companion on fishing trips, too, and she spies the fish in little pools before I do. She comes with me to Devon, where on summer dawns we take a boat out to sea and fish for mackerel, Ella safe in her little dog life jacket.

Then, after we have landed and filleted the fish, she shares my freshly caught breakfast, cooked over a campfire. If I'm seeing someone, I don't book nights away in hotels. Instead I'll take my potential girlfriend on walks – even if it is in driving rain – and, should things go that way, I'll pitch a tent or rent a cottage so that Ella can enjoy the adventure too.

These are the outings Ella and I prefer. We don't covet luxury and we hope the company we choose will enjoy the untamed outdoors too.

I start to feel that Ella has, in her quiet way, started to appraise my girlfriends. There is one very chic French girl – we'll call her Marie Claire – who arrives for a weekend walk in a Scottish glen dressed as if for a city break in Paris.

There are a group of us in hiking boots and jeans; she, meanwhile, tiptoes along in her unsuitable shoes, yelping with annoyance when she stubs her toe on a boulder or snags her smart coat on a bramble.

When we come across a pool flanked by trees and big enough to swim in, we boys strip down to our boxer shorts and dive in. Ella follows, thrilled by the prospect of a dip, her nose just skimming the waterline as she paddles into the icy depths.

Much to our surprise, Marie Clare decides to join us. To our collective amazement, she strips off all her clothes and poses at the water's edge stark naked before diving elegantly into the pool. As she hits the freezing water, she lets out a shriek of astonishment and scrambles out with an indignant squeal.

Ella has already decided that Marie Claire is not the woman for me. If a girl does not like hiking and cold-water plunges then she won't be a good fit. Ella seems to sense, too, when affection and attention is genuine. She can spot a fraud from twenty paces. She does not warm to those who feign fondness for her. She is the dearest of dogs but she can be quite aloof if she thinks that someone is just pretending to like her.

There is no ambivalence with my sisters: she adores Catherine and Pippa and knows the love is reciprocated. So on the occasions when we decamp from Edinburgh to London to join them in our family's flat in Chelsea, she is as delighted as I am.

It is early in 2010. I still have a toehold in Edinburgh but spend more time in London now, where Pippa and Catherine are not too thrilled to have their little brother disrupting their orderly, tidy existence, strewing damp clothes over the bathroom floor, leaving unwashed crockery in the sink and letting Ella pad wet-pawed across the living room carpet. But they bustle round in their kind, sisterly way, clearing up after their messy little brother with only the mildest of rebukes.

Ella has one antisocial habit. She loves to roll in fox poo. And because our flat has no outside area or garden hose, I have to wash her in the bathroom. Quite often we sit in the bath together and I scrub and shampoo her. I realise now how infuriating this must have been for my sisters: the tidemark of grimy water; dog hairs clogging the plug.

On one occasion I use every towel in the house to dry her, and these are circling round in the washing machine or draped over clothes airers when Catherine and Pippa get home.

Despite my lack of house training, my sisters are protective of me, and prefer me to be with them than on my own. They can keep an eye on me, make sure I'm getting up in the morning. And they're equally glad that Ella is with me, because they know she is my prop, my comfort; actually my reason for being.

By now, William has been dating Catherine for six years, so I know him well and there is no scramble to clear up when he comes to supper. But I remember putting him through his paces when we first met. Did he deserve my sister? He had to earn my trust.

It helps of course that William is so genuinely fond of Ella. When he first encountered her as a tiny puppy at Bucklebury he was smitten. He'd had a black Labrador, Widgeon, when he was a boy, and when Widgeon died he left an empty space. I felt William was pining for a dog when Ella was around.

I know, too, that Ella gives him a good excuse to escape the fiercely competitive nature of the Middleton family, which emerges every time we play our favourite fast-paced card game, racing demon. It involves multiple decks of playing cards and is often described as a more cut-throat form of patience or solitaire. Our family have enjoyed it for generations. My paternal grandmother was so good at it that even in her early eighties she would thrash us.

William flinches at our ruthless determination to win at all costs. He's delighted to be the first out, and when no longer compelled to take part, he slinks off to cuddle Ella. I think he'd prefer to absent himself from the game entirely.

'James, does Ella need a walk?' he asks before we've even started dealing the cards. My sisters and I exchange a knowing glance: William, for all the competitive rigour of his military training, is happy to be a loser at cards.

I saw a lot of William when he was an officer cadet at Sandhurst, which is fairly close to Bucklebury. So by the time I'm toing and froing between Edinburgh and London, he's become part of the family.

The paparazzi pursue him and Catherine tirelessly, and I lose count of the times I breeze out of the front door to find a sea of photographers on the doorstep, bitterly disappointed that it is me, rather than William, emerging blinking into the sea of flashing cameras.

Sometimes I'll be walking back to our flat late in the evening when an officer in a police protection car, parked discreetly up the road, alerts me to the fact that William is visiting, and Ella and I will make an extra loop of the block to delay our return.

On the rare occasions when I go away without Ella – perhaps I'll be taking a flight – she enjoys staying with Catherine and William. I give them a long list of dos and don'ts, but I know she is a reliable dog and I can trust her. She would never run off, jump up or forget her manners.

But there is always guilt – and most of all, a sense of missing her – accompanying the trips I make without her, so I try never to leave her.

Ella, ever equable, takes it all in her stride. My family are dependable, loving, loyal, but Ella's instincts are now so finely tuned that she feels part of me and knows me in a way that perhaps even outstrips their sense of me. She recognises my moods; knows when to be gentle and calming and when she can lark and play.

When we walk together, she stays close. She does not need a lead. Even in a field of sheep she is at my side. If she trots ahead of me, she always stops to look back for my approval.

The best walks are just Ella and me, with this unspoken communion between us. I'm not hugely sociable – my friends are loyal but few – and I'm happy with my own company as long as Ella is with me.

So this is how it begins, I think, when my invitations start to become addressed 'To James and Ella'.

I'll often be invited to dinner parties and I'll send my apologies: 'I can't come because I don't want to leave Ella alone.' So then the reply comes: 'Do bring her with you.'

I take her, and because she is a sweet-tempered, well-mannered dog, my friends warm to her. The idea percolates through them all: James will accept invitations if he can bring Ella with him.

The fact is that, thanks to Ella, I am more sociable. Because of her, I strike up conversations with strangers in the street. The subject I love most is my dog, and if others share my enthusiasm, we enjoy happy impromptu chats.

She comes with me to the dentist, and although she isn't allowed into the consulting room, the receptionist is delighted to let her sit unobtrusively under the desk while I'm having my teeth examined.

She even comes to business meetings in London. I've evolved a foolproof strategy for getting her in. At the last moment I call and say, with breezy self-assurance: 'Oh, by the way, I have Ella with me.'

I don't actually mention that she's a dog, and invariably no one will ask, 'Who's Ella?' So when I arrive, no one has the temerity to turn her away.

It's thanks to Ella, in fact, that I don't become a recluse. She is my plus-one, my constant companion.

Chapter Three
An Audience of Two Billion

———

We're at a boathouse on Windermere, a primitive hideaway with a boat stashed underneath and a single room above.

I'm still in that transitional phase between student and worker bee, gown and town, Edinburgh and London, and the Lake District is midway between the two cities, my two lives.

Sometimes I'll meet friends here, six or eight of us, girlfriends and boyfriends, but I'll choose Ella as my travelling companion and nestle up to sleep with her on the boathouse floor. In the morning we'll be first up for a stroll.

Walking has been a constant in my life, and my greatest walks to date have involved human companionship. Pippa and I climbed Mont Blanc and the Matterhorn together; as a family we'd trek for miles in the Alps.

But here we are now, just Ella and me, discovering a dawn-fresh landscape and wildlife together with a child's sense of awe and wonderment. Ella notices the hedgehogs, shy and self-contained, who only bristle when interrupted. She is gentle with them as I have trained her to be.

I am confident she will not badger them; she rewards that trust by watching their scuttle from woodpile to leaf mound from a respectful distance.

She is a great observer of nature, and we sit in silence and listen attentively to its sounds: the rustles, the birdsong.

While she is still small, I take an old rucksack of Dad's with me, and when she's tired she sits in it and I walk in time to the rhythm of her breathing, the steady beat of her heart.

These trips are a solace, a time of meditative quiet, and I value them. Because – although I do not recognise them as such at the time – I am experiencing early signs of the mental health problems that will later threaten to consume me.

Back in Edinburgh, I have acid reflux so often and so disconcertingly that the doctor sends me for endoscopies. He wonders if I have a stomach ulcer. Are you anxious? he asks. I shrug off the suggestion. But of course I am.

I'm trying to set up my fledgling cake business, but my parents are still insistent the right option for me is university. How can I make a success of myself without a degree? is their constant refrain.

It does not help my cause that Pippa has a 2:1 from Edinburgh and Catherine also has an upper second from St Andrews. The girls set a high benchmark, but I always just plodded along, and Mum and Dad, who expect similar academic success from me, can't understand what they perceive as my lack of ambition.

Acutely emotionally aware, I absorb their anxiety.

The school system I went through offered me no alternative to university either. But I know that, if I continue to pursue the degree path, I'll fail, and three precious years will have been wasted.

So once again I tentatively suggest to my parents that I might not be ideally suited to academic study. I begin by testing the water over Sunday lunch, tiptoeing round this potential landmine of a conversation by inventing a friend who has given up his degree course to pursue a business career.

My father is not impressed by this hypothetical friend. 'Well I guess he'd have to pay his own rent and his car insurance would be very expensive,' he speculates.

Mum weighs in to enumerate all the positives of being at university: the limitless horizons it opens up, the discipline and rigour it instils, the lifelong friendships forged.

Over the course of a few months I drop more hints about leaving, all of them unfavourably received. Then, when I finally admit to my parents that although I'm shuttling between London and Edinburgh I'm not actually studying for my degree any more, they cut off my financial support.

Dad is exasperated, Mum tearful. Neither of them understands why I'd choose to throw up this opportunity to further myself in life. So it's non-negotiable. No university, no money from the Bank of Mum and Dad.

To follow my own path, I have to stand on my own two feet financially, so I'm determined to make a success of the cakes.

My best friend, Nick, helps me write my business plan. I show it to my godfather, Uncle Gary, Mum's brother – an entrepreneur – who likes the idea. He invests a few thousand pounds, which gives me a flying start and buoys me.

I bid on eBay for a static catering trailer and trundle up to Manchester to collect it. Then I set about converting it – I'm grateful now for my practical skills, learned tinkering as an adolescent – so that it's food-safe and I can make my cakes in it.

I know that Ella can't be with me while I'm baking, so I make a little annexe for her, with a window in it so she can sit and watch me work.

My kit cakes are selling well and I develop a method of printing photos onto cupcakes. I'm proud to tell anyone who asks: 'I left university to become a baker.' I find myself supplying cupcakes to glamorous events in London.

During London Fashion Week, I'm invited to a string of parties for which I've supplied the cakes. But socially – away from the production line – I'm at sea, floundering in a milieu that is completely alien to me. I arrive at Ralph Lauren's party in jeans, a ripped shirt, odd socks; the same clothes, actually, I wore the day before to traipse through the woods with Ella.

There are splashes of mud and dog pawprints on my trousers.

I do not feel at ease among the social butterflies, the gorgeously clothed, the fashionistas. I am on the edge, not absorbed into the scene but an observer looking on.

There is a terrific buzz throughout the country at the time because the rumour is spreading that Catherine and William are about to get engaged.

Of course our family know a day or so before it is officially announced in November 2010. Catherine, Pippa and I go out for a walk with Ella and Tilly to our local pub in a village close to Bucklebury.

We sit in a corner, chatting quietly, catching up on our lives. Catherine whispers the news and says it will become public in the next day or so. Pippa and I want to be visibly excited, but we have to tamp down our emotions so that no one suspects a thing.

We make a quiet acknowledgement that we'll always be there for each other, look out for one another, support each other. No matter how crazy things get.

William has been in our lives for so long and we've grown very fond of him. He feels like our older brother and he and Catherine are so clearly a good fit, just right for each other. I haven't yet experienced for myself the kind of love they feel for each other, but I'm hoping that one day I will.

Now our first priority is to keep their secret for 48 hours. Mum and Dad know, of course, but we don't discuss it again. We've learned to keep confidences close.

On the morning it is going to be announced, Catherine rings to let me know. I walk with Ella in Battersea Park, savouring the secret knowledge and feeling a thrill of happiness for them.

I remember tramping for miles with Ella that day and returning to our flat via Sloane Square Tube. The first edition of the *Evening Standard* was piled high. There on the front page was a picture of Catherine in her blue dress. I tucked a copy under my arm and walked home with a sense that it was all quite surreal.

I thought how lucky William was to be marrying my capable, down-to-earth big sister, and I felt absolutely reassured that they were in love. It was beautiful to see how he brought out her confidence. She'd blossomed. I knew he'd look after her, and he does to this day.

The royal aspects of William's life were incidental; an intrusion even. They were living in Anglesey, where they would spend the early part of their lives together. But I don't think any of us were prepared for the huge surge of interest in our lives that their engagement brought, and the adjustment that came with it.

Tourist buses would cram into our street in London as curiosity about even the tiniest minutiae of Catherine's life grew. They'd stop at the door of our flat and we could hear the tour guide's commentary declaring in ringing tones over the microphone: 'This is where Catherine Middleton lives.'

I'd keep a lookout for them, peeping out of the front door to make sure the coast was clear of tour parties before emerging into the street. If I was spotted, I knew I'd be nobbled: 'And here's Catherine's brother James making a dash for cover.' I got pretty good at dodging the paparazzi too.

I was quite naïve at the outset though, and I quickly learned how cut-throat some sections of the media were in pursuit of a story – any story, however inconsequential – about my big sister.

There was no official rule book, but William would make useful suggestions. And his constant mantra was, 'Be careful.'

There were times when I got things wrong.

I posted a photo of myself wearing a polka-dot dress one Halloween, and someone somewhere got it into their head that it was Catherine's dress. It wasn't. It belonged to a friend. No harm was done on that occasion, but I started to be more circumspect about the photos I shared. And I realised how even the most trivial stories assumed disproportionate importance.

Was anyone really interested in me wearing drag on Halloween? Apparently – and unaccountably – they were.

Meanwhile the baking business was doing well, and I made the back-to-front commute from our flat in Chelsea to Bucklebury, where I worked all day in my food trailer, extending my repertoire of cakes from five to twenty-five designs.

The buzz around the engagement generated further interest in my growing business, and an order came in from a chic Paris hotel. They wanted 2,000 cupcakes on a specific afternoon and a further 4,000 to follow. My excitement at securing such a thrillingly large order was eclipsed by the fact that I'd nowhere near the capacity to make such a vast number of cakes in my trailer. And then there were the logistics of transporting them.

Everything had to be done perfectly – I didn't want to let the new French customer down – but I realised that I'd have to seek help.

So off I went to see my friends, baker Fiona Cairns (who later went on to make Catherine and William's wedding cake) and her husband Kishore Patel, in the Midlands. I was bubbling with excitement and thrilled to see that they had the capacity to bake the cupcakes in their factory.

The deal was struck: they'd make the sponge and I'd take charge of the decoration.

But the manufacturing of the cakes, it emerged, was the easy bit. Transporting 2,000 cakes across the Channel was as challenging as a military operation.

Dad had an old 1988 Renault van, and because I was operating on a shoestring – and wanted to personally ensure that my precious cargo arrived safely – I begged him to let me borrow it so I could drive the cakes to Paris myself.

He grimaced. 'That van hasn't travelled more than ten miles in the last decade,' he warned me. 'But I suppose you can use it if you want.'

Thrilled, I measured up, calculated that I could get everything in the van and prepared to take the 2 a.m. Eurotunnel shuttle (the cheapest one) across to Calais.

Ella would normally have been with me, but I needed to update her vaccines for her pet passport, so reluctantly I left her with Mum and Dad and rattled off – ignoring the ominous graunch and clatter from the engine – to catch the train.

I reached France safely, but four miles outside Calais I ground to a halt, oil pouring from the engine, smoke billowing, just managing to steer off the road and onto a verge.

And then I realised that I had no mobile phone signal.

I sat there, panic rising, thinking, 'What do I do? What do I do?' The sun hadn't yet risen, and even the feeble blink of my hazard lights was fading as the old battery wore down. And the cupcakes! Elaborately festooned with buttercream decoration, they'd start to melt once the day warmed up.

Fortunately for me, the French are diligent about monitoring their roads, and a passing tow truck spotted me and pulled over. The driver got out and I addressed him in my halting schoolboy French.

Could he help me get back to Calais? I wheedled. If he could take me to the van rental place there, I'd give him the Renault as payment for his trouble because – small extra encumbrance – I hadn't got any cash.

'*Rien du tout*,' I emphasised, turning out my empty pockets – at the same time imagining Dad's appalled reaction when I told him his van had breathed its last in France and I'd traded it in for a lift.

But my pleading didn't wash with the truck driver. He had a different plan. He told me he'd take me to his breakdown garage, leave my van – and its cargo of cakes – there, then drive me to Calais.

So that was what we did. At the rental place in Calais, I asked the hatchet-faced woman behind the counter if I could hire a van. She looked at me as if I'd presented her with a particularly bloody specimen of roadkill. ''Ow old are you?' she asked.

I murmured my age, 23. And here was yet another setback: I wasn't old enough to be entrusted to hire a van. I can't tell you how desperately I didn't want to ring Dad to ask him to help me out, but this seemed to be the only solution.

I'm happy report that Dad speaks French fluently. I don't quite know how the conversation went – perhaps he just pleaded with the woman to take pity on his accident-prone son – but ten minutes later, I was on the road in a smart new rental van, having signed an insurance waiver and paid an extra-high premium in case anything unforeseen should happen.

Humming a happy (relieved!) tune, I set off through the meandering lanes back to the garage where I'd ditched my first steed. The chain-smoking owner was already sitting in his tiny office.

'You have my van,' I reiterated brightly, gesturing magnanimously to the defunct Renault. Having promised it to him when he rescued me at the roadside, in lieu of payment for the lift, I was determined to honour the pledge.

'Where are your papers?' he growled.

'I don't have them,' I said lamely.

There was nothing for it: he insisted I write him a cheque – *and* leave him the van. It seemed a high price to pay, but I was determined to redeem the disastrous day and deliver the cakes.

And there was something fitting about leaving the vehicle on home ground. Dad's trusty little Renault, having spent its entire life on British soil, had felt the Gallic air rushing through its carburettor and decided it had come home to die.

Waving a last wistful goodbye to the van in which Dad and I had shared many childhood adventures, I set off again for Paris.

Despite this unforeseen three-hour delay, because I'd left home so early I still – just – had time to get there with my delivery.

When I found the chic hotel, in a charming cobbled back street, I was ready to turn cartwheels. Despite all the setbacks, I'd managed to get there. Cakes unscathed.

'I've got a delivery,' I announced with all the pride and relief a midwife must feel when presenting a newborn to its parents.

'Then go to the tradesmen's entrance,' came the sharp rebuff.

So off I trundled – only to discover that the service lift wasn't working and I'd have to carry my trays of cupcakes up the stairs to the ballroom.

Nobody knew the effort, expense and nail-biting tension it had taken to get those baked goods to Paris, but my customer was delighted – the cakes were intact despite the detours – and this felt recompense enough for the epic journey.

But then there was the small matter of how I'd get home. Flying, I'd calculated, would be cheaper than driving and taking the train, so I dropped the hire van at the airport – more surcharges, as I hadn't driven it back to base at Calais – and tried to buy an air ticket . . . only to find that my credit card had been cancelled because of 'suspected fraudulent activity'. (Well, I had forgotten to tell my bank I was going abroad.)

There was only one thing for it. Dad to the rescue. Again. I phoned home and could almost feel the effort it took him to bite back the chastisement: 'I told you so.' Yes, he had warned me. Yes, he had questioned whether the van was up to a 500-mile round trip. And yes, he would sub me the fare home.

So I got on the plane – minus the van and 2,000 cupcakes – clutching just my passport, and finally arrived back on UK soil at Heathrow airport 24 hours after I'd set off, where the welcoming faces of Mum and Ella were waiting for me in arrivals.

After paying Dad back, I calculated that I'd made a profit of precisely nothing, but the cupcakes had been a success and the hotel still wanted 4,000 more. So Fiona and Kishore baked them and I decorated them – but second time round, with valuable experience gained, I arranged for a professional delivery company to transport them.

The wedding was barely eight weeks away when Catherine and William, on the phone together and bubbling with excitement, asked me brightly if I might be up to doing a reading on their big day at Westminster Abbey.

A reading? I thought they were joking. My mind raced back to school and my stumbling, incoherent efforts to read in front of the class. What *were* they thinking? Being dyslexic, reading is my least favourite occupation. Why would I risk my humiliation in front of the entire world?

Ask me to do anything else – groomsman, page boy, even flower girl! – and I'd have done it willingly. In fact I'd rather have spent the day before the wedding cleaning the Abbey floor with a toothbrush than contemplate reading aloud a passage from the Bible.

'Seriously?' I asked.

'Seriously,' they chorused.

Oh no! I thought.

'No problem at all!' I fibbed breezily, while thinking what an enormous – possibly insurmountable – problem it would in fact be.

But if that was what my sister and William wanted, then of course I'd do my best not to let them down.

Then they added: 'This will be the only Bible reading in the service,' and I didn't know whether to be honoured or appalled.

Over the next few days I tried in my mind to lessen the importance of the role. 'Don't think of it as a royal wedding. Just imagine it's your sister's wedding at the local church,' I told myself.

I was sent the reading – Romans 12:1–2, 9–18 from the New English Version of the Bible – and I carried it with me everywhere I went, taking it out of my pocket to practise the lines, over which I tripped and stumbled, transposing syllables, getting my ps and bs – my nemeses – in a twist.

Then, terrifyingly, Catherine rang to say that I'd been given the wrong version of the reading. The one they wanted was more complex, with more poetic cadences. Not the King James version, but the New Revised Standard Version, which the Abbey used.

'You can still say no,' she reassured me, but I was loath to disappoint them.

'Fine! I'd be delighted,' I fibbed before I had time to censor myself.

And so it was that I was committed to doing a reading in Westminster Abbey before a packed congregation and a critical world watching at home on their TVs.

Then Anthony Gordon Lennox came into my life.

Anthony, by chance, lived across the road from me in Old Church Street, Chelsea. He was often described as a 'voice coach', but that did not do justice to the magical alchemy of his approach to teaching public speaking.

He had helped David Cameron when he was PM, and his method was to make those he was tutoring reveal their humanity and vulnerability; their authentic voice.

Very kindly, he offered to help me out too. I remember the evening he called me, the relief I felt, and the dissipation of the panic that had gripped me.

The film *The King's Speech* had come out a year or so earlier, and I'd watched it feeling empathy with King George VI, whose stutter had been cured by the speech therapist Lionel Logue. I felt Anthony would assume a similar role with me. Just the thought of his presence was calming.

Anthony came to our flat one evening and asked me to read the lesson out loud. I could see from the expression on his face that I had a lot of work to do.

I said to him: 'Will you read it to me? I learn better that way.' And when he did, the whole thing suddenly made sense.

I practised reading it myself in the flat, in front of Anthony. And practised again. I wrote the whole text out phonetically so I wouldn't make pronunciation blunders. Then I needed a bigger venue to rehearse in, to get used to the ecclesiastical acoustics.

Fortunately I knew the vicar of the nearby church, so one evening Anthony and I knocked on the rectory door and asked if we could borrow the church for some out-of-hours rehearsals.

Everything had to be kept under wraps. 'It's for a friend's wedding,' I prevaricated. The vicar smiled and nodded. He would be delighted to lend us a key, he said, and we could pop by when we wanted and lock ourselves in while I practised.

Of course I took Ella along to rehearsals with me. She sniffed around, politely acquainting herself with the place, probably looking for a wafer of communion bread. And she became my audience.

Anthony told me to present my reading to Ella. As she pottered around the church, my gaze followed her. If I'd fixed my eyes on a single point, Anthony said, I'd have seemed robotic. But Ella was keen to look around; her inquisitiveness, in turn, helped me relax.

It was a new experience, too, because I was – for the first time – speaking into a microphone. The reverberation was disquieting, distracting. For a while I was completely thrown. But I grew accustomed to it.

Back at the flat, I practised again and again, declaiming from my now crumpled sheet of phonetic text. Ella sat patiently on a chair in front of me and I spoke to her. I'd occasionally put her name into the reading so her ears would prick up. I knew when it was time to stop, because after a while she would sigh with exasperated boredom.

Actually, said Anthony, I would need to learn the words by heart. On the day, the text would merely be a prompt – I wouldn't actually be reading it.

I recorded myself doing the reading, and on long walks with Ella I'd listen to these recitals, alert to ways I could improve, analysing every nuance of tone and volume. Sometimes I'd recite verses out loud as we walked, then try them again with a different emphasis.

Ella looked at me quizzically, as if she thought I was going crazy, but my aim was to give a reading that was faultless yet seemed relaxed and spontaneous. And this involved hours and hours of patient practice.

'Don't rush,' said Anthony, and this was vital. Nerves can make you hurry, and I needed to slow down.

There was only one chance to rehearse at Westminster Abbey, and this was on the evening before the wedding. I arrived on foot because there was so much traffic. Roads were being closed and cordoned off; diversions were set in place.

Ella, of course, was with me, imbuing me with a confidence I would not have felt without her. I hesitated at the steps to the Abbey: would she be allowed into this sacred place?

Fortunately she was, and there was someone willing to sit with her and hold her while I ran through the crucial timings: an usher would meet me at my allotted time in the service, and I'd walk to the lectern and begin . . .

I asked for a copy of the reading and scanned it. To my horror, two words had been changed. This was enough to send me into a spiral of panic, but Anthony reassured me. 'Don't worry. It's too late to change your version now. Just say what you've always said. No one will know.' He smiled.

He was there with his stopwatch. Everything had to be timed to the second. Would I finish at the right moment? Would I lose my nerve? Would I acquit myself well on the day and make my sister proud? All these thoughts converged on me as I stepped up to the lectern.

I looked round as I stood there, spotted Ella, smiled. Every eye was on me. I wanted to laugh, but I counted to four and the giggle subsided. Then I noticed the echo, far longer and more resonant than in the church where I'd practised.

As I began – 'I appeal to you, brothers and sisters, by the mercies of God, to present your bodies as a living sacrifice, holy and acceptable to God, which is your spiritual worship' – the bustling Abbey fell still.

At the end, as I walked back to my seat, Anthony was there smiling. He was happy, and I will be forever grateful that he was able to give me this invaluable help before his premature death in 2017. 'Well done,' echoed Huw Edwards, who would be commentating for the BBC on the day, and was there for the rehearsal, before adding, 'Make sure you keep to that timing. And ensure you give us enough time to introduce you before you start.'

This did nothing to quell my nerves, and the glare Anthony gave him spoke volumes. 'Do not put him under any more pressure,' his look said.

When I went to retrieve Ella, who had attracted a posse of admirers all wanting to stroke her belly, I felt she was delighted too, not least because the responsibility for listening to the reading hadn't rested solely with her.

But tomorrow, I reminded myself, Ella wouldn't be with me. It would just be me, a packed Abbey and a worldwide TV audience of about two billion people.

Chapter Four

Newborns, and a Calamity at Bucklebury

———

I am as prepared as I can be. More rehearsals would be counterproductive, so I just try to concentrate on keeping calm.

It's Catherine's day of course, not mine, and there are so many little details to attend to. They are a welcome distraction.

Ella is with me at the Goring Hotel, a stone's throw from Buckingham Palace and the Abbey, where our whole family is staying on the night before the wedding.

She is just what I need to quell my nerves. I take her for an evening stroll, walking down through the lobby, which is bustling with activity. The final tweaks are still being made to Catherine and Pippa's dresses late into the evening.

Strangely, although everyone is busy, there is an aura of complete calm, belied by the look of intense concentration – sometimes even mild panic – on their faces. Everywhere I look, something is happening. There are dresses, hung on racks, being steamed in one room; further down the corridor someone is speaking intently into their walkie-talkie. The conversation stops abruptly as I walk past.

There is so much to absorb. On TV screens in the hotel I watch the coverage from news teams all over the world who are stationed on the pavement outside, updating their audiences on what they think might be happening inside. It makes me smile, listening to their speculation as I amble in the midst of it all.

Ella and I find a quiet area in the garden to potter round. There, a replica of Basil's Bar in Mustique – a small private island in the Grenadines and a holiday spot the family had visited many times – has been set up. Basil himself is to be one of the wedding guests.

Basil's story is a colourful one. A native of the nearby island of St Vincent, he spent a year recovering from a motorbike accident and was then offered a job as a barman by Colin Tennant, later Lord Glenconner, who then owned Mustique. In 1976, he took charge of the bar on the water's edge that Colin had named after him.

Today Basil's Bar has become the social heart of the island. Mick Jagger, Jon Bon Jovi and Bryan Adams have all played in this unassuming little venue on the water's edge.

Now a perfect facsimile of it has been built in the grounds of the Goring Hotel so wedding guests can imagine themselves on the edge of the Caribbean while actually in the middle of a London garden.

Ella and I take it all in, and I chuckle to myself that she has managed to visit the bar before any of the other guests. Then it is time for her to come back in for her supper.

She is only allowed in my room and the garden; even so, I worry about black spaniel hairs finding their way onto Catherine and Pippa's dresses.

Ella is very good about not jumping onto beds and sofas, but she senses my jittery state of mind and, I'm sure, knows I have a momentous day ahead of me tomorrow. So as a special boost to my morale, she (illicitly) jumps onto my bed and falls asleep curled up beside me.

I'm relieved that I sleep quite well. Next morning my biggest headache, as I dress carefully for the day ahead, is getting my tie straight. Looking back at photos now, I see that it has a kink in it, but at the time that feels incidental; far less important than remembering to take my worn and crumpled phonetic copy of the reading as my prompt.

This well-read piece of paper has accompanied me everywhere, scrunched up in my pocket, for the past eight weeks. It has been folded and refolded a hundred times and annotated with squiggles and in highlighter pen with notes only comprehensible to me. But it is like a child's comfort blanket. It makes me feel safe and secure.

Some well-meaning person on the wedding roster offers to retype it for me on a pristine white page. 'Oh no!' I almost wail. Without that prompt I will be lost.

It tells me when to look up and down; when to soften my voice and be more emphatic, when to pause and breathe; in fact how to make the whole meticulously rehearsed performance seem absolutely natural and uncontrived. I hand it over, assured that it will be placed on the lectern for me this morning.

I remember walking into the Abbey – awestruck all over again by the grandeur and magnificence of it – and revelling in every moment of the service. There is so much to absorb. Then, far sooner than

I expected, there is my cue. Someone has glided up to me, silent as a shadow, to take me to the lectern.

I walk steadily, trying to calm my breathing. I stand, poised to begin. But where is my scruffy piece of paper? I can't see it. Has it been thrown away? Is it languishing in a bin somewhere? Panic almost overwhelms me.

Then I turn the page of the Bible in front of me, and there it is. Someone, obviously thinking it lowered the tone, had concealed it. Relief washes over me like a balm.

I wait until the great Abbey falls silent. Ten, perhaps even fifteen seconds. Then I count slowly to four and everything that could possibly go wrong floods into my mind. Are my flies undone? Will I have a coughing fit? Will my voice squeak or wobble?

I try not to be too consumed by the vast scope of the occasion. I pretend it isn't a royal occasion. It's just my sister's wedding and she's asked me to do a reading.

I don't even cast a glance at Catherine and William, not wanting to exchange smiles with them in case I erupt into nervous giggles. I want to do them both proud.

I glance up and see happy faces I recognise in the congregation and the nervousness falls away.

I take a deep breath . . . and begin.

And then I'm speaking the words as if to an intimate church full of friends: 'Let love be genuine; hate what is evil, hold fast to what is good; love one another with mutual affection; outdo one another in showing honour.

'Do not lag in zeal, be ardent in spirit, serve the Lord.'

They come back to me now as if I spoke them only yesterday.

When I get into the flow of the reading, I actually enjoy it. I left the television on in my room at the hotel to keep Ella company, and I imagine her sitting there in front of it, watching the coverage, ears alert as she recognises my voice. Then, hearing me speak the words that have become so familiar to her, I picture her putting her paws over her ears with an inward yelp of 'Oh, not that old thing again!'

Later, with the reading successfully over, after all the wonder of the day, the service and the celebrations, all I want to do is throw on a pair of old jeans and take Ella out for a walk.

I also remember thinking: 'I'll insist my sisters do something on my wedding day.' I joke with them that I'll be putting them down for a flute duet and they'd better get practising.

Ella and I went back to Bucklebury the day after the wedding, and it was work as usual the following week.

It wasn't until then that I allowed myself to think about how momentous the day had been and realised just how many people had watched the ceremony on TV.

It was the largest audience for a Bible reading ever. I received thousands of messages from well-wishers and invitations to read lessons at churches around the globe that would have given me scope for a Bible-reading world tour.

In a different spirit entirely, I was also invited by an American production company to star in my own movie. The letter, on important-looking embossed paper, suggested a fee of $1 million as an 'opening offer', and even ventured that members of my wider family might like to take part.

It made me laugh – what a preposterous thought – and I filed it away in my box of mementoes and vowed to frame it and display it in the loo when I bought my first house.

It was coming into summer 2011. I still had links with Scotland, and my girlfriend at the time was performing at the Edinburgh Fringe. I thought I'd surprise her with a visit, so I flew up, full of excited anticipation, and waited outside the venue until her show had finished, relishing the thought of how delighted she'd be to see me.

As she walked out, absorbed with something on her phone, I rang her. 'Watch out or you'll walk into that lamp post,' I said, adding, 'I'm right behind you.'

She turned round, looked appropriately surprised, then burst into tears . . . but not in a good way.

And then it all came tumbling out.

She'd been seeing someone else, someone in the cast. My romantic surprise had backfired calamitously. An hour later, I was on a bus back to Edinburgh airport, embarrassed that the same flight crew were there for my return journey as the one out, trying to sound matter-of-fact when I explained to them it had just been a quick trip.

When I got home, Ella looked at me with mild reproach in her eyes. 'Next time, take me with you,' they seemed to say. I imagined her thinking: 'I always knew she wasn't right for you.' In fact, her sixth sense about girlfriends was unfailing. She'd never particularly warmed to this one.

The wedding had also given fresh impetus to my cake business, and the invitations to bake for society events all over London almost overwhelmed me. With them came a slew of cheery requests to turn up to launch parties and openings, drinks dos and PR events.

Frankly, I didn't want to go and once again used Ella as my excuse. 'I've got a dog. I don't like to leave her alone in the evenings,' I'd prevaricate. 'Oh, do bring her too!' came the inevitable response. And Ella got even more invitations to go to smart parties all over London.

Going on my own to these events would have been excruciatingly difficult for me, but Ella made them bearable because she helped break the ice. Most people warm to a well-behaved dog, and Ella would never impose herself on anyone. She'd wait to be greeted then enjoy being stroked and fussed over.

Then, inevitably, the conversation would turn in the direction of my favourite topic: dogs. I could talk about Ella endlessly – and if I ever needed to make a getaway for any reason (if people were taking drugs; if I didn't feel the atmosphere was comfortable), I'd use her as a reason to leave. 'I need to take Ella out for some air,' I'd say, and off we'd trot, never to return.

She became my litmus test. If Ella was welcomed and made to feel at home, I would feel at ease with the company. If she wasn't, I'm afraid I didn't want to go.

At that time, taxis were loath to take passengers with dogs. They'd drive away if they saw Ella at my heel. So often we'd end up walking home together at night. Once we got locked in Hyde Park and I thought we'd be sleeping there, but I managed to scale the huge iron gates carrying her on my shoulders.

She was my companion in every type of adventure, and pretty soon I took her on her first flight – to see her dad, Zulu, on Islay.

I got her accustomed to the crate she'd be travelling in long before we took the flight itself, and on the day, I took her to the cargo area hours before the plane was due to leave. But when a forklift truck arrived and her crate was strapped onto a pallet and lifted skywards onto the truck, I started to worry.

'What have I done?' I fretted. I'd heard, and tried to block out, horrific stories of animals perishing of cold in the hold because the captain hadn't looked at the manifest to check that they were on board. So I refused to sit in my seat until I'd confirmed – via the cabin crew – that the pilot was aware Ella was there.

I was so relieved when I heard him say, over the public address system: 'This is your captain speaking. Heater on in the hold. Don't worry.'

Then there was all the drama of disembarking a dog. Where would she be? How would we be reunited? No one seemed to know. Then someone told me she'd be on the luggage carousel. I had visions of poor Ella going round and round like an unclaimed suitcase.

But then she emerged in her crate from a doorway by the baggage belt, and as she was wheeled out, I heard a rhythmic whacking on the side of the container. She was so excited, so delighted by the whole experience, and so pleased to see me, she couldn't stop wagging her tail.

I'd been poised to comfort her, to tell her how sorry I was, but there was no need. Far from being traumatised, it appeared that she had enjoyed every minute. And so a new chapter began. Ella got her wings and became quite the seasoned flier.

Soon after she turned three, she had her first litter of pups. I did lots of research into spaniel lines to see who would be the best match for her, then, in the middle of a winter snowstorm, went to Wales to meet Peter, an experienced breeder, who had a dog called Spartan who might make a suitable boyfriend for her.

Peter, stocky and bearded, is an eminent figure in the dog world. A Kennel Club judge since 1992, he has been trialling cocker spaniels (taking them to competitions) for 40 years. I whispered to Ella as we approached his house, 'We have to be on our best behaviour.' I knew his own spaniels would be models of obedience and I wanted to prove that Ella was a match for them. Dutifully she trotted by my side, casting me the occasional glance so I could smile my approval.

Peter was clearly both passionate and knowledgeable about spaniels. He spent a long time studying Ella's bloodline, and such was his expertise and insight into the breed, he even knew the characters and temperaments of her forebears. He concluded that Spartan would make an ideal match for her.

I watched as he talked to his dogs, issuing his commands just once – they complied instantly – in a voice barely above a whisper. 'Spaniels have very good hearing,' he explained. 'There is never a need to raise your voice. If you have to shout, something is wrong with the way they've been trained.'

The introductions successfully completed – Ella could not have acquitted herself better – we agreed I should return with her when she was ready.

So I took her back at the appropriate time, she met Spartan and I left her with him for 24 hours.

After that, all you can really do is hope. It seemed that everything had gone well, and as a dog's gestation period is only nine weeks, it isn't a long wait.

After four weeks, I took Ella to the vet for an ultrasound scan. And there, nestled together like tiny ping-pong balls, were a cluster of pups. She was pregnant!

I hadn't actually told Mum and Dad about the imminent new arrivals, or that I intended they'd be born at Bucklebury. How to communicate the fact without getting into trouble with them? I had a brainwave. I stuck the photo of Ella's scan on the fridge door, knowing Mum would be horrified, thinking I'd got a girlfriend pregnant, and that it would soften the blow if I could then say, 'No, they're Ella's pups!'

My ruse worked. There was an audible sigh of relief from Mum as she peered at the fuzzy, indistinct image and I told her she was soon to be granny to a batch of adorable puppies.

Like Dad, Mum was very fond of Ella, and I'd often catch her furtively reading my books on dog breeding and checking Ella for any signs of distress.

'James, are you sure you know what you're doing?' she asked as I cleared out the boot room to make it into a nursery for the impending arrivals, and I assured her with a smile that I did.

Five weeks on, I knew Ella was almost ready to have her litter, because she wouldn't let me out of her sight. She watched me closely, padding behind me whenever I left the room.

That night, I stayed up with her and encouraged her to go into her whelping box (a designated space for dogs to give birth and raise their puppies), but she wouldn't stay in there unless I was by her side, a comforting arm placed on her.

I remained in the box with her, dozing fitfully – there wasn't enough space for me to lie down, so I sat upright – until at 3 a.m. I was woken by her panting. Clearly she was in labour.

By the time I'd fully woken up and, every bit as nervous and excited as any expectant first-time father, reached for my book on whelping, Ella had given birth to her first pup. She'd bitten open the sac that covered him and was licking him clean. I thought then how incredible her maternal instinct was. Without any help, she was doing exactly as she should.

Forty minutes after the first pup came another, a boy, then after another interval, a third, a fourth and a fifth – all boys. All were settled and happily feeding by the time Mum and Dad came down the next morning.

Ella must have been exhausted, and she fell asleep as the pups suckled while I refuelled on a bacon sandwich. She left her litter momentarily to eat her breakfast, but as soon as one squeaked, she trotted back to the box to check on them.

For the next six weeks she looked after them until they became independent; their hazy grey-blue eyes starting to open after ten days, then their ears. Gently she encouraged them when, after three weeks or so, they started to walk like wobbly toddlers on unsteady legs.

She trusted me to handle them, and they were growing more confident and sociable when Catherine and William came to see them. 'Would you like one as a belated wedding present?' I asked. 'All you have to do is choose your favourite.'

There in the box nestled the five glossy black pups. Catherine and William bent down to stroke their tiny muzzles. But they needed to discuss the practicality of having a puppy first. They would be going to live on Anglesey, where William would work as an RAF helicopter pilot at the Coastguard Search and Rescue base.

I reasoned that a puppy would be company for Catherine on the nights he was away on duty. They were won over. And after much deliberation they settled on a pup they called Lupo.

At eight weeks, Lupo left his mum and, to Catherine and William's delight, went to begin his new life with them in Wales. I, meanwhile, kept another of the pups, Zulu, named after his grandfather.

Once word got out that I had three other male pups that did not yet have homes, my phone started to ring. 'Hi, James, how are you doing?' began the first enquirer, who, within seconds, had moved on to the real purpose of his call. 'Any chance I might have one of Ella's pups?'

Like an overprotective parent, I vetted every caller carefully, assessing their suitability. Did they have the right lifestyle? Would their job allow them to give a dog the attention he deserved? Would they love him unconditionally, be patient, kind and attentive? My list grew shorter after each interview until I had whittled it down to two local friends we'd known for years and an old school friend.

All of them, I concluded, would be loving, conscientious dog parents, and once the pups were ready for independent lives, off they went to their new homes.

Much later, when Ella had her second litter, I told Pippa's then boyfriend James that I was sure she'd love a pup too. He asked me which of the batch was her favourite, and I picked out Raffa.

So it was that Raffa became my middle sister's dog – to this day I'm convinced the pup was instrumental in sealing their relationship.

In the summer of 2013, Catherine was preparing for George's birth. She'd been spending more time at Bucklebury because she had acute morning sickness – hyperemesis gravidarum – for the whole of her pregnancy and Mum was looking after her while William was away working as a search and rescue pilot.

I was still doing the back-to-front commute from the family flat in Chelsea to work in Berkshire, and sometimes I'd pop in to see Mum, Dad and Catherine. It was a glorious summer and the whole world, it seemed, knew that Catherine was pregnant, so people were constantly asking: 'Any news?'

As the day of the baby's arrival drew closer, the activity ramped up a notch at Bucklebury. A stream of visitors came and went.

Then early one evening, a couple of weeks before Catherine's due date, I was driving back to London from work when my mobile rang. There was Mum's familiar number, but the voice on the end of the line was a stranger's.

Over the crackling of static, I could just make out a couple of disparate words – 'accident . . . dog' – interrupted by staccato jolts of silence. I didn't wait to hear more. The surge of panic was instantaneous.

I sped through the winding country lanes back to Bucklebury, overtaking a car and noting that it stayed close on my tail all the way to Mum and Dad's. It screeched to a halt as I did and a posse of officers jumped out: it was an unmarked police car. My heart was pounding as I took in the scene: a fire engine, blue lights flashing. I abandoned my car on the road, leapt out and ran towards the electric gates of our house.

There was Mum, one arm soaked in blood, vainly trying to calm a distressed and frantically wriggling dog whose head had become stuck between the gatepost and the gate. Dad had a crowbar and was trying to widen the gap so the dog could be freed. Meanwhile the fire crew was figuring out its own strategy for releasing him.

And the trapped dog was Ella's pup Zulu.

Mum, trying to contain her distress, explained what had happened. During the afternoon there had been much toing and froing. The gates had opened and closed several times to admit visitors.

Zulu, who had been playing in the garden with Lupo, seized the chance for a bit of mischief. As the gates opened again, he put his head in the gap, perhaps in pursuit of a squirrel. Then when they swung closed, the space in which his head was lodged narrowed to the width of two fingers.

He started howling. His neck was being crushed. Mum, alerted by the commotion, had rushed out and tried to keep him still so he didn't wriggle and snap his vertebrae. Distressed, Zulu had bitten her. Now his yelps of pain were growing weaker as the minutes ticked by.

The fire crew decided to cut through the gatepost with a chainsaw, but I was worried that the noise would scare Zulu so much he'd try to wrench his head free, with catastrophic results.

So I grabbed another crowbar, and Dad and I managed between us to apply enough leverage to split the metal post.

Gently I pulled Zulu free, holding his head and body tightly against my chest. By now our wonderful vet, Mark, had arrived and was ready to take us to his surgery, where an emergency team were waiting.

As he drove, I cradled Zulu in my lap and we discussed our options. We agreed that Zulu would be dispatched straight away for an X-ray, and if his neck was broken, I would make the awful decision to have him put to sleep.

The journey seemed interminable. Zulu's small body went tense, then limp. His eyes rolled to the back of this head; his tongue lolled. I held him tight and he would resist, then all his energy seemed to ebb away.

At the vet's, his heart stopped beating, but a shot of adrenalin revived him and it started to pump again. Next he was sedated so he wouldn't move.

He was taken for his X-ray, and I remember stepping out of the room and realising only then that I was covered in blood. Zulu had managed to bite through his tongue while he was stuck in the gate.

My restless pacing – anxious, aimless – continued while I waited for news. Zulu was being stabilised, tubes sprouting from his inert body.

My phone kept pinging with well-meaning messages: how is Zulu? What's the prognosis? But I was too choked with worry to respond.

Eventually Mark emerged and I almost burst with relief when he said, 'I can't immediately see a break, but we have to get a specialist involved and do an MRI scan.'

So Zulu was prepared for this more detailed diagnostic scan and kept in overnight for observations and monitoring.

Heavy-hearted, I left him there and returned to the commotion at home. The fire engine was just leaving; our doctor had arrived to check Mum. Zulu had not bitten her out of anger, but because, gripped so tightly to restrain him, he felt stressed.

Still, that didn't lessen my guilt about Mum and worry about Catherine, who wasn't fully aware of what had happened. I lay awake that night, restless and anxious, watching the minutes tick by into hours as I thought about Zulu and what the outcome might be.

The vet called early. Zulu, still sedated, was ready for his MRI scan. Then back came the results. Jubilation! There was only bruising of the cartilage. No break. But he'd been lucky. He'd been half a centimetre away from a crushed neck.

Even with this lesser injury, his recovery was slow and painstaking. His neck was swollen, and the swelling meant that less blood could reach his spinal cord and nerves. As a result, neither could get enough oxygen. The focus was on getting the swelling in his neck down as quickly as possible so he didn't suffer permanent damage.

Mark agreed he could come home, and we turned a downstairs room at Bucklebury into a temporary field hospital for him. He lay on his bed in his cage, just able to hold his drooping head without support.

A bit of mobility was good; too much would hinder him. Mark taught me how to do some physio on his legs and tail so we would be self-reliant and I could help him convalesce.

Bit by bit he learned to push himself up into a sitting position, but his hind legs would not support his weight and dragged behind if he tried to walk. So – channelling my boyhood DIY skills – I made a little harness from an old rucksack, wood and staples to support the weight on his rear legs so he could start to walk again.

Meanwhile, George had been born at St Mary's Hospital in London and Catherine was back at Bucklebury. Both of us would wander round at night – she to feed George, me to check on Zulu – and we welcomed the chance for a chat in the early hours.

There was a time, too, when his injury made Zulu incontinent, so both Catherine and I were changing nappies.

It was ten months, during which time I was working while staying at Bucklebury, before Zulu completely regained the use of his legs, and several more before his muscles had built up to full strength again. But finally he was restored to fitness; nobody would know he'd suffered a bad injury but for the sensitivity around his neck. It still distresses him today to have a lead and collar put on, so we treat him very gently.

During the months when he was recuperating, he spent a lot of time apart from the other family dogs, in my father's office. The two of them built up a strong bond that persists today. Sometimes I smile quietly to myself and think: Dad never wanted a dog, but look at the two of them now.

He'd find special treats for Zulu, and bought him a new dog bed. Once I caught him tucking him in for the night. Sometimes he'd even introduce him to friends as his own dog, and if I gently teased him about it, he'd pretend not to hear.

We all bond with our dogs and Dad had formed a special alliance with Zulu that was wonderful to see. That's just one of the many miraculous things about dogs. They forge different relationships with all the people who love them and learn quickly the rules that apply with each of them.

Before long, Bucklebury had returned to relative calm. Catherine left with George, who was still quite small when she and William packed up their home at Kensington Palace and set off for Anglesey with Lupo in tow.

I have cherished memories of visiting them there with Ella when George was still a baby and going for bracing walks along clifftops and across vast golden beaches with Catherine while William was at work. We consulted the tide timetables and watched the ebb and flow of the sea, but one day, engrossed in our walk, we nearly got stranded, only saving ourselves by taking a long detour and getting back to their cottage after nightfall.

Their life together in their seaside cottage with George seemed idyllic, and I remember thinking: 'I can't wait to meet someone and have my own family.' I chatted to Ella about it as I always did, sharing my thoughts and wishes.

'When that happens,' I told her, 'I'll feel complete.'

Chapter Five

Ella's Royal Walkabout

———

Pippa and I were late for Catherine's birthday party, which in the normal run of things wouldn't have mattered too much, but this time the Queen had kindly offered to host the teatime gathering at Sandringham, so it was crucial we arrived on time.

We'd been on an overnight flight to Gatwick from France and had arrived bleary-eyed and sleepless at the airport, then I'd driven us both to Bucklebury so we could pack. I was fretting about the standard of my ironing – my shirt was rumpled and creased in all the wrong places – and I could only find one cufflink.

'Come on, James, we've got to go now or we'll miss tea,' urged Pippa as I filled up Ella's water bottle for the journey. (Zulu, still recuperating, was staying at Bucklebury with our parents' housekeeper.)

Cursing every traffic jam on the journey, we arrived breathless and flustered with barely time to run upstairs and change. I was hopping into my shoes and tucking in my shirt as I raced along the corridor. Then I bounded downstairs two at a time and into the room where everyone was assembled for tea, almost running smack into Her Majesty. She and Prince Philip had got up to leave just as I blundered in with Pippa behind me.

All the way up to Norfolk I'd been rehearsing my lines, muttering 'Your Majesty' for the Queen; 'Your Royal Highness' for the Duke of Edinburgh. But in my blind panic I blurted: 'I'm so sorry we're late, Your Royal Majesty.'

I heard snorts of laughter and looked past the Queen to see everyone in the room stifling giggles.

'Oh, how lovely to see you, James,' she smiled. I'd met her several times, notably at my sister's wedding, and she was always welcoming. 'You must be hungry. Make sure you have something to eat,' she went on serenely as she continued her regal progress out of the room.

I blushed fiercely and peered into the drawing room to see the whole family grinning at me. Pippa was pleased that the focus had been on her hapless little brother rather than her. Mum gave me a resigned smile and came over to hug me, straightening my crooked tie as she did so – which reminded me that I'd forgotten my bow tie for the evening (though this being a well-appointed household, a spare one was found and brought to my room).

Whenever we visited Sandringham, the Queen, being a dog lover herself, welcomed Ella, and one year after Christmas, Tilly and Zulu came too. Her Majesty was always concerned about their well-being, and knowing the special place Ella held in my heart, she allowed her unprecedented privileges.

'Did you get my message, James?' she asked me the first time I visited. 'Ella is welcome to stay in your room.'

I couldn't contain my surprise and delight. How thoughtful of the Queen to make a special concession for Ella. Naturally she wasn't allowed to wander at will round the grand house, so I kept popping up to check on her and take her for walks.

On one visit I didn't close the bedroom door properly, and Ella, unaware of the protocol, made it her mission to find me and demonstrate her annoyance at being left behind. I didn't realise this until a footman glided up to me and whispered, 'I believe your dog has found her way into the kitchen.'

I quickly made my excuses and followed him to find a delighted Ella lying on her back, having her tummy rubbed by a friendly chef.

'We thought she must be Lupo,' he smiled, and I explained that she was, in fact, mum to Catherine and William's dog. After this little foray, we trotted back to my room and Ella settled back on her mat.

Ella, I'm slightly embarrassed to record, made quite a habit of ambling off during family occasions. One Christmas I popped into Highgrove to visit Catherine and William, who were staying with Prince Charles.

Catherine and I were having a catch-up over a cup of tea, with Ella sitting at my feet. After I while I realised that she had wandered off, obviously feeling comfortable in familiar surroundings.

When I went upstairs to change for dinner, she still hadn't materialised, so I asked one of the household team if they'd seen her. 'Don't worry,' came the reassuring reply. 'We'll keep an eye open for her, but she won't have gone far. It's no problem.'

So, assuming Ella was having a sniff round the grounds, I got dressed and went down to dinner.

It was then that I learned that she had, in fact, made her way up to a private bathroom and had pushed open the door to say hello to the occupant as they were having a bath. I was absolutely mortified, particularly as I was trying to be on my best behaviour and wanted Ella to oblige by being a model of canine decorum too.

But I couldn't quell her mischievous streak. And when the bather came down to dinner, they seemed amused that they'd had a visit in their bathroom from a black spaniel. They assumed it was poor Lupo. I didn't want to dob Ella in and get her into trouble, so I stayed judiciously silent on the matter.

And I'm pretty sure they remained none the wiser.

I didn't imagine the Queen would ever find out about Ella's little adventure into the Sandringham kitchens either, but nothing escaped her. She said to me, 'I hear Ella had a nice little wander round earlier,' and I apologised profusely, expecting a gentle telling-off.

Instead, with the understanding that comes from long association with dogs, she gave me a conspiratorial smile and said, 'Well, dogs will be dogs.'

Everyone knows about her corgis, but few are aware that she also had a line of spaniels. One lunchtime we became engrossed in a long conversation about them, and I was thrilled to discover she was extremely knowledgeable about the breed.

She was always kind and solicitous about my dogs. 'Have you taken Ella out, James?' or 'Are your dogs happy?' she'd ask with genuine concern.

At Sandringham Christmases, we joined in the family gathering. Beatrice and Eugenie, whom I knew from school, would be there and we'd all go to church in the morning.

One year the Queen and I sat down to do a jigsaw puzzle. It was the sort of activity I'd have enjoyed with my own grandparents, all four of whom had died in the space of three years when I was a teenager. So in a way, I felt the Queen was filling a granny-sized void in my life.

And there we were, engaged in this everyday pleasure, which was elevated to the extraordinary by the company I was in. It still feels surreal, the fact that I was there with the Queen: I look back on it with amazement.

She frequently put down five pieces to my one, deft-fingered while I was inept, scanning the board with practised eyes, not even stopping when people came to talk to her, but still chatting as she slotted in the pieces. I hoped she wouldn't notice how little I contributed.

Once we'd finished the jigsaw, she asked if I needed to check Ella, and I went to walk her round the grounds, trying not to look as if we were up to mischief, hissing at her to get off the flower beds.

There were presents, too, modest but wrapped with care. Mine from Her Majesty was a pair of socks; I gave her a card with a photo of Ella on it and a few jars of my own honey, which I brought down to breakfast on Christmas morning.

The Queen talked to me about beekeeping and I knew she appreciated the effort it takes for a colony of bees to produce enough honey for a jar.

I've been a passionate advocate of these ingenious, industrious little creatures since I became a beekeeper nearly a decade ago, having fallen for them as a child. I now have almost half a million bees in eight hives in a meadow at Bucklebury, and I'm in awe of them.

They perform a little waggle dance, an insect version of sat nav, to signal to each other where the best flowers are. They'll fly up to five miles a day to seek them out. And the sheer industry of their daily task is boggling: in a worker bee's five- or six-week lifespan she will produce just one tenth of a teaspoon of honey. That's ten bees' lifetimes to fill a single spoonful. So, knowing her Majesty would be aware of how much effort goes into producing the liquid gold, I knew she'd appreciate the honey.

Honey is one of the few foods that never spoils – there are samples dating back thousands of years. It is nature's finest medicine: it aids digestion, helps alleviate cold symptoms and hay fever, provides a slow-release form of natural sugar and is even said to promote restful sleep. I've read, too, that it has a role in alleviating depression. And of course it tastes delicious.

But more than that, bees – some species of which are endangered and vulnerable – pollinate food crops and are vital to the delicate balance of the earth's ecosystem. Insect pollination is worth £690 million to UK crops alone each year.

There are so many reasons to keep bees, aside from the quiet, immersive pleasure of looking after them. I love spending time with my bees, checking, monitoring, treating them and collecting their honey: it is soothing toil; a comfort for troubled minds.

Hives are highly organised communities presided over by a queen bee. So a jar of honey, a gift from a queen to the Queen, seemed fitting.

By now you understand me well enough to know that I always warm to people who love dogs and go to places where dogs are welcomed.

Even when she was not expressly invited, I took Ella to social events as my plus-one. One year at the *Harper's Bazaar* Christmas party, she slipped off in search of mischief and I discovered her in the midst of a circle of adoring revellers. She loved being in the thick of things. Then, in the magazine's next edition, there was Ella with the editor, lapping up the attention.

Ella started to become a media star, a dog about town. *Town & Country* magazine wanted to write a profile on her, with photographs. She willingly acquiesced. She was a sociable dog, and while I am shy and reticent, she adored fuss and the limelight.

Had I given her the chance, I know she would have attended every party in London. She became an honorary member of every club we visited. And Ella was the reason I felt at home at 5 Hertford Street, a private members' club in Mayfair, where canine visitors were treated like VIPs because the owner, Robin Birley, was a great animal lover.

In the historical tucked-away building, dogs were allowed to sit on the chairs. In fact, if they'd commandeered an armchair, they took precedence over humans, who weren't allowed to oust them.

Ella was already beloved by lots of the staff there, so it was a delight to take her along and see her stretch out in front of the fire or jump onto her favourite chair and be fussed over by the team.

Often I'd get back from work, put on a jacket and smarten up a bit, then amble along with Ella from Old Church Street to Mayfair via Hyde Park – a lovely walk – to meet friends for a couple of drinks.

I was trying to budget at the time and couldn't stretch to eating there, so I'd fill up on the complimentary bread sticks and nuts on the bar, then, still needing a meal when I got home, drop off at the 24-hour supermarket for some pasta and pesto.

But Ella was treated royally at 5HS. The kitchen staff would give her slices of chicken breast and carrots doused in rich gravy, which she'd eat with relish. I remember thinking: 'I wish I could have some too,' as I contemplated my solitary bowl of pasta waiting for me at home.

On one of my visits to the club in the winter of 2013, I met the actress and TV presenter Donna Air. I'd no idea who she was – much later, I realised she'd played Charlie Charlton in the kids' TV show *Byker Grove* – but we started chatting about animals and she clearly loved them, so that shared passion was what drew us together. We talked late into the evening, exchanged numbers and decided to meet up again.

Our friendship grew into a relationship that went on for four or five years. I kept it quiet for a few months, telling neither friends nor family, but in that intuitive way of close family, they knew I was seeing someone.

We had fun. Pippa had moved out of Old Church Street by then and I was cooking dinners for Donna, trying to impress her with dishes I'd made myself but usually messing them up. I remember picking up a fresh fish from the fishmonger, who asked if I wanted him to gut and scale it.

Being a bit too confident in my own abilities in this regard, I told him blithely that I'd manage quite well, thanks. After all, I'd fished in the Lakes and in Scotland many times and had gutted the catch and cooked it on a campfire.

Much different, I discovered, when you try it at home. Finding that Pippa had taken most of the decent cooking utensils (to be fair, they were hers), I made a complete hash of it, hacking at the fish with a blunt knife and covering every surface in the kitchen with scales.

So I abandoned the fish and went out and bought a very expensive takeaway curry from a nearby Indian restaurant instead, then failed miserably to pass it off as my own.

Luckily Donna laughed when she saw the foil containers I'd hastily stuffed into the kitchen bin, and was as happy with a takeaway as my idea of home-cooked fine dining.

After a few months, when we couldn't keep our relationship a secret any longer, she came home to Bucklebury with me for the weekend and I introduced her to my family. Mum was delighted I had someone in my life, but although she really liked Donna, she had misgivings about our relationship.

Donna was eight years older than me and had a daughter, Freya, then aged ten, by her former partner, Damian Aspinall. I liked the fact that she had a family life and roots. Actually, I found it stabilising. But my parents cautioned me about the age gap.

Their hesitation actually convinced me even more that I wanted to be with Donna. Meanwhile we discovered that we had lots of mutual friends, and spent weekends together socialising.

But Ella, always nestled between us, started to show signs of jealousy, muscling in when we sat together. She never really saw eye to eye with Donna's Lhasa Apso either, and I suppose that might have been a sign that we were not meant to be together.

Was I happy? I think I convinced myself I was. But looking back, I was losing control. My mum's reservations about my relationship with Donna made me all the more determined to pursue it. But I was in a limbo of indecision, terrified to commit but scared of ending it. The push and pull of it was isolating.

It was the early days of my new business too, and work was getting busier and busier. My cake company had evolved into Boomf. The idea came to me because customers had started to ask if we could deliver our cupcakes through the post.

The notion of a cake being posted through a letter box and landing with a splat on the floor didn't seem workable. Much better, I thought, to come up with an edible product that would be more easily sent through the mail.

So I invented a way of printing photos on marshmallows, which could be posted with greetings messages.

I'd been thinking: what noise does a marshmallow make when it falls through a letter box? *Boomf* seemed to be the closest approximation. So the company name was born. I had a fantastic partner, the business was growing quickly, and we were winning awards for the best Christmas and Valentine's gifts. It was an exciting time.

I'd started with cakes because it felt like a natural segue from everything I'd seen of the family business, but it was my love of inventing things that found a creative outlet in this new venture. I evolved a printer, cobbling together parts of different machines, to print the photos. I spent weeks in the kitchen making marshmallows from gelatine, sugar and water, with cornflower as a setting agent.

The temperature had to be precisely right so they weren't too sticky; the amount of cornflower crucial so they didn't set too firmly.

Ella was with me throughout the whole experimental process, often covered in corn starch when I rushed and dropped a bag. She was my companion as I worked into the early hours trying to perfect a smooth marshmallow ideal for printing photos on, which could be transferred directly from Instagram.

The marshmallows were a success. Customers were ordering faster than I could produce them, so I found a manufacturer who could make sheets of them that were then cut into bite-sized squares ready to be printed on.

Within a few months, we'd moved into a vast warehouse that was soon bursting with scurrying staff dispatching thousands of marshmallows. At peak times we were working 24-hour days.

We were invited to have a stand at Selfridges just before Christmas. Long queues of customers waiting with their photos to be printed on personalised marshmallows were forming.

The printing machine was working overtime, and sometimes it would glitch so I'd be called in to fix it. One night I was driving back from work and got the by now familiar call that it had broken down.

So at 10.30 p.m. I found myself, in high-vis jacket with a lanyard round my neck and armed with a head torch, outside this grand department store ready to get to work.

I managed to sneak Ella in, and she sat quietly under the counter until 4 a.m., when, having finally fixed the fault, we made our exit, breezing confidently past the security guard. 'That was a very long evening. We're off now,' I said, as he looked on, confused as to what a man and his spaniel could possibly have been up to all night in an empty department store.

Other times weren't such plain sailing. After one particularly gruelling night fixing the printer, I was just packing up to leave when I knocked over a pot of blue food colouring. As it hit the floor, I heard the ominous *glug, glug, glug* of its contents spilling over the pristine tiled floor of the upmarket shopping mecca.

Cyan food colouring is a particularly stubborn dye to erase, and I looked on helplessly as it pooled across the floor and under counters.

Rushing to the rest rooms to grab all the available loo roll and dam the encroaching blue tide, I heard a faint beeping from an upper floor and recognised it as the sound of an industrial ride-on floor cleaner.

This would be my salvation! All evidence of the dye would be erased by the cleaner and no one would any be the wiser. I followed the beeping and found its source. Once I had explained to the machine's operator that there had been a dye disaster downstairs, he kindly agreed to help me clean it up. He also directed me to the janitor's cupboard, where there was an assortment of mops and buckets.

Then off he trundled to assess the spill. He decided he should drive over it repeatedly, thereby vacuuming it all up. But that only made it worse. The stain seeped outwards, creating a blue wash everywhere he went – and the more he rode over it, the more stubborn it seemed to be.

The sea of dye spread and spread and I had visions of Selfridges opening and staff arriving to find the entire floor suffused in a blue tint.

We abandoned the bright idea of using the machine, and having scrubbed it clean as thoroughly as we could, we returned it to its cupboard, both of us pledging to keep the whole escapade a secret.

Then I got to work wiping and mopping the floor. Vast department stores are eerie places at night – the echoing emptiness in stark contrast to the bustle of day – and I cut a strange figure scrubbing away in my suit and tie, made marginally more obtrusive by a bright yellow high-vis.

A golden dawn broke over Oxford Street, and as the first of the staff arrived for their day's work, I emerged blinking into the daylight. People stared at me in mild disbelief; this odd figure, baggy-eyed with tiredness, his hands dyed blue, trundling out of the store as they walked in.

Ella had spent a comfortable night, meanwhile, snug in her bed in the car with regular visits from me for pee breaks and little walks. We drove back to the office as the great city stretched its arms and began its day.

I didn't recognise it at the time, but during this period when work was demanding and I'd often be called out to fix broken machines, my mental health was declining.

There is no real logic or reason as to why this happened, but although the business was thriving, I'd started to lose confidence in myself. I tried to mask it and took up lots of physical challenges to distract myself. Pippa and I cycled across America. I ran marathons. I thought I'd drive out the negative thoughts on an endorphin high of exercise.

A group of three friends invited me to Burning Man (so called because a large wooden effigy of a human is burned at the end), a celebration of art and self-expression in the Nevada desert.

I'd never been to a festival before, though I'd often caught the distant blare of a rock band drifting across the fields to Bucklebury from Reading, and I wondered if I'd be cool enough, but I was reassured by the word 'art' in the description, and the more I read about it, the more excited I was about going.

Visitors to the festival bring no money and everything is bartered, so I hit on the idea of trading peanut butter and jelly sandwiches for other necessities.

We booked a recreational vehicle in Los Angeles – every RV closer to the site was already taken – and a friend and I (only two of the four of us had the relevant documents) took turns to drive this bus-sized behemoth the 600 miles to the mudflats where the festival was held.

On the way we bought 30 loaves and a dozen or so jars of jelly and peanut butter, then, arriving at the festival, got to work making the sandwiches and freezing them. Luckily the RV had a well-equipped kitchen with all the appliances we needed.

The sandwiches proved a hit; we swapped them for drinks and everyone was in high spirits.

Usually I'd be the first to wake each morning and would go out on my bike – the site was so vast we all cycled – leaving a note on the door assuring my friends that I'd be back soon, but invariably I'd get sidetracked by a conversation or an adventure and arrive back hours later.

I ambled in and out of tents, chatting to their occupants – young parents, children, elderly couples; there was no stereotypical 'type' – and watching performances.

I got caught up in the relaxed spirit of the place. I revelled in the freedom. No mobile phone reception. No paparazzi chasing Donna and me. It was a wonderful escape, and I whiled away hours sitting on top of the camper van looking out at the vastness of the desert, sipping tea and reflecting on life.

There was a bat squeak of recognition that something was wrong within me, but I didn't know what it was. What I did know was that the time away from 'real life' had made me reflect on what I valued most. I returned with a mission to focus on what was important in my whirlwind existence, but faced again with the reality of work and relationships, the aim was subsumed.

The reprieve of the desert was only temporary. Even when I was surrounded by people I felt alone. And I was gripped by this awful inertia. I didn't want to accept invitations because I feared it would all become too much for me and I'd have to cancel at the last moment. There was no rational reason why I couldn't agree to anything – even to lunch with my family, an outing with my sisters – but I refused to engage with anyone.

The business was continuing to prosper, but I struggled to find it exciting. And although I was extremely fond of Donna, I kept cancelling arrangements to go out with her. I couldn't give any logical explanation for it. But I became more and more insular and Donna was understandably irritated by my failure to commit to a relationship with her.

Depression – I now know this was the condition that was causing my inertia – is draining. I felt perpetually exhausted, and what little reserves of energy I had I put into working.

When friends called to invite me out, I'd make excuses. Their insistence made me even more adamant. I'd just say I couldn't go.

I continued to train and go to the gym – keeping myself fit was an imperative – but there was no pleasure in it any more. I walked the dogs, but took no joy as I once had in the changing seasons, the beauty of the world around me.

Then I started losing sleep. I tried to remedy this by continuing to push myself physically, running marathons, cycling, undertaking endurance races. Nothing helped. I didn't want to see anyone because I felt dull. The colour had ebbed out of my life. Everything was black and white. And I had no idea what was going on.

I withdrew into myself. I did not answer phone calls, failed to reply to emails, never responded to a knock at the door.

The lack of communication with anyone, even those closest to me, was understandably creating problems with my family and friends, with work and with Donna. And the more effort they made to reach me, the more insistently I pushed them away.

A new CEO took over the business, which relieved me of some pressure, but I was losing control of myself and everything around me.

Catherine and Pippa became more and more worried about me. They would invite me to go and see them – we'd have everything planned – then at the last moment I'd cancel. And because I could not give them a cogent reason why, they'd get perturbed.

They'd feed back their concern to our mother, who would phone me and say: 'Why didn't you go?' and I'd be touchy with her because she was challenging me. My only explanation was that I couldn't do it.

On the rare occasions when I did meet someone, I would be restless. I'd take Ella with me, of course, and after 40 minutes or so I'd get an uncomfortable feeling. There was nowhere else I needed to be, but I felt this terrible compulsion to leave. It was a constant sense of anxiety and insecurity, similar to that sense of panic you feel when you're about to miss a plane. So I'd find myself rushing off and then saying to Ella: 'Where are we going now? What was that all about?'

Even if I was at the cinema, I'd walk out in the middle of a film, consumed by anxiety and this urgent need to leave. The problem was that I did not know where I wanted to be. There was no respite from this awful restlessness.

Exercise was my only solace. I could go for a run, push myself; get a temporary break from the horrible sensation, the void at my core. But I was on a downward spiral.

I lost weight. I couldn't eat. Ella alone gave my life structure and form.

She'd had another litter of pups and I had kept two of them – Inka and Luna. The daily rituals of feeding and walking them gave me purpose even as my life was disintegrating.

But the torture was the chasm between outward appearances and reality. Everything about my life looked perfect – a flourishing business, beautiful girlfriend, loving family – but inside, my mind was in chaos and I had absolutely no idea why.

Chapter Six

My Descent into the Abyss

———

A dog's death is profoundly different from a human's. When a beloved human is dying, you can express your love for them and they can reciprocate. If there is time, you can reflect with them on the happiness you've shared, the accumulation of memories. This communication is a solace.

But a dog's passing pulls at different heart strings. There is no two-way conversation, just the dull weight of a grief that can never be imparted in words. The lifespan of a dog is short. It always feels as if a dog dies too soon.

Tilly was an old golden retriever, approaching 17. Although she was on medication, she was struggling to walk. But there was still a wag in her tail and an alert look in her eye. And she still had her appetite, a good sign.

Mark had already warned us that her back legs would give way or her vital organs would fail. 'Be ready for it and we'll make the appropriate call,' he said.

But of course you never are quite ready. If a wolf in the wild is ill or injured, it detaches itself from the pack, goes off alone and falls asleep under a tree. It chooses a solitary death so it does not imperil the rest of the family by making them vulnerable to predators.

Dogs share 99 per cent of their DNA with wolves, and it gave me a shred of comfort to think that Tilly, if she had been alone in the wild, would have known when her time had come. So the consolation was that if she had to be put to sleep, she would not suffer the agonies that humans do. It would be us – her family – who would grieve.

As Tilly was nearing the end – and to fill an approaching void – in the autumn of 2016 I decided to breed from Inka. I'd found a suitable mate and we thought she was pregnant. But she wasn't putting on weight, so off we went to Mark again, where an ultrasound scan suggested that the mating had been unsuccessful. These things happen. I resolved we'd try again.

Then one evening Inka went missing. I searched all her favourite spots but couldn't find her, but as I walked back to the house feeling perplexed and worried, there she was at the door – with a puppy held carefully in her mouth.

So she'd been pregnant after all and this tiny puppy, tucked away inside her, had managed to evade the ultrasound scan. There was no sign that she'd given birth to any others. I felt guilty, panic-stricken. How could I have missed the signs?

I found an old suitcase and got to work making a whelping box, which I filled with bedding for Inka and her pup.

Off we went to Mark to get Inka checked over, and because she wasn't producing milk, he gave her an injection to encourage lactation.

Inka's pup was so tiny that a diminutive name seemed appropriate. I called her Mini. I also knew I'd need to help feed her, so I set my alarm to wake me every three hours during the night and fed her warmed puppy formula through a pipette. This vulnerable little creature fitted into the palm of my hand, and I was desperate for her to survive.

For the next four weeks I shared the feeding with Inka, and then we weaned Mini onto solids. She was still small but seemed healthy. She slept snuggled in the suitcase, which was convenient, because everywhere I went I'd take her with me. The suitcase was the perfect portable whelping box.

Mini continued to thrive, so I started to think about finding a new home for her. I had wonderful friends in Sweden who were very keen to have a pup from Ella's line, and I told them about her little granddaughter.

They came to meet her and said how delighted they'd be to have her. I arranged her vaccinations and passport. In six months she would be ready to travel to her new home.

But she wasn't gaining weight, and by the time she was four months old, I could tell that something wasn't right. Checks at the vet's revealed that her heart wasn't growing at the same rate as her body. Mark told me she'd struggle to reach adulthood; that the kindest thing to do would be to have her put to sleep.

Mini was five months old. Inka and I had nurtured her; she had already become great friends with Ella. Her character was just starting to develop. It was devastating holding her as her tiny heart was stilled.

Inka was subdued, and I'm certain that she was grieving for her dead pup too. Her maternal instinct had never left her. Whenever I'd fed Mini, Inka would jump up on the sofa beside me, her head in my lap, licking my hand and her pup.

Her gentle, nurturing nature persists to this day. She can carry a chick in her mouth with such tenderness it does not flinch or feel fear.

I buried her pup in the garden near the spot where, three months later, I would bury our beloved Tilly.

We all knew Tilly's health was declining, but in the serendipitous way that often happens in life, new hope was springing. I was driving back from Scotland with Ella when my phone started pinging. I pulled into a lay-by to see if it was urgent and listened to a message.

'Hi, James, you probably don't remember me. It's Jude. I was just speaking to your mother and I wanted to let you know that Tilly's great-great-granddaughter has just had eleven pups. I had to share the happy news!'

A couple of puppy photos popped up. Cute as buttons.

I rang Mum. 'Have you spoken to Jude?'

'Yes, I was going to talk to you about it.'

'Let's chat when I get home.'

All the way home I was wrestling with the thought: could I justify having a fifth dog? Was it a remotely good idea? By the time I reached Bucklebury, I'd convinced myself it definitely was.

Mum wasn't so keen if it involved too much commitment on her part, but I took matters into my own hands and the next day called Jude.

'If there's a chance of a girl pup, I'd love to come and meet them.'

Jude said she'd be delighted, and we agreed to wait until the pups, then only a few days old, were more mobile before I went to visit. Tilly, meanwhile, got slower and older.

A few weeks later, I drove to Southampton to meet the pups. I fell in love with one in particular – I can't tell you what drew me to her – and Jude, who could identify each one, promised to keep her for me.

Back home, I announced to Mum, 'I've decided, I'm definitely getting a puppy.' She sighed heavily. But knowing how devoted I was to Ella and my other dogs – and they to me – she realised there was no point in resisting.

Knowing that Tilly's days were numbered, I didn't want to leave her, so I resolved to stay at Bucklebury with her for however long she had left. I sat with her, stroked her old head and told her I'd chosen one of her great-great-granddaughters to come and live with me.

I like to think that she knew there was a new golden retriever coming – one of her bloodline, too – and that she could smell the puppy (whom I later named Mabel) on me. And so, conscious that a new pup would soon be nipping at my heels, I told myself that when Tilly's time came, she would slip away contentedly.

By now she was less responsive and just wanted to sleep all day, so that night I decided to sleep downstairs on the sofa next to her bed. I woke early, cramped and uncomfortable, and looked across at Tilly beside me. I stroked her head again, felt for a breath or a sigh. She did not wake.

My parents were just rousing from sleep when I went up to their bedroom, and I could hardly articulate my grief. 'Tilly has passed away,' I said through my tears.

Mum and Dad came downstairs and we began to make plans to bury her, the beloved companion of my childhood. Our dear family dog, steadfast, gentle, true.

There was one corner of the garden Tilly had loved. It was where she would always hang out because she could see the door of the house and our comings and goings, and she'd sit there for hours. It was near the tennis court, too, where she loved to fetch balls whenever we played. So we figured it would be a lovely place for her grave.

I started to dig, but as my spade hit the ground, the emotions flooded in. Everything collided: my grief at losing Tilly and the realisation – now impossible to ignore – that, perfect though my life seemed to the outside world, nothing was right.

As much as I tried to bury the fact, as I dug her grave I felt as if I was digging myself into a deeper metaphorical hole. I asked myself: was all this grief for Tilly? I was distraught, certainly, to lose her. But there was an unidentifiable sadness there too.

I'm ill-prepared for the enormity of the loss, for the sheer blank emptiness of my grief.

Nothing gives me joy any more.

It is the first time I acknowledge that there is something fundamentally wrong with me and that possibly Tilly's death is the catalyst.

The last goodbye is the hardest part. As I stroke her silky ears one final time before the cold earth covers her, the tears are pouring down my face.

When I look back now, I think the deaths of first Mini, then Tilly tipped my already fragile mental health over the edge. But still I don't know what is happening to me.

Although I acknowledge to myself that all is not well, I don't want to admit it to anyone else. Concerned friends ask, 'Are you okay?' and I assure them I'm fine.

Then my sleep, already poor, starts to completely disintegrate. My thoughts are constantly churning and I cannot process them. There is no respite from them. At 2, 3, 4 a.m. I'm wide awake yet exhausted, trying to still the tumult in my mind.

I look for advice on the internet. Write it down, put it on paper, is the consensus. So I try. And when I read back the incoherent jumble of my thoughts, they seem even more incomprehensible and strange.

My relationship with Donna is suffering too. For a while we separate.

I've read about depression, but I do not acknowledge I could have it. What can I possibly be depressed about? The idea that I could have problems with my mental health does not cross my mind.

But it is as if I'm walking through a bog: the more I try to extricate myself, the more I am sucked down into the morass.

I can't think any more. I'm tired of thinking. I don't know what makes me happy. My dogs, particularly Ella, are my only source of comfort.

By then our new golden retriever pup, Mabel, has come to live with us, and my mother loves her. She brings new life to the house and we decide we'll share responsibility for her. Mum is delighted with her new companion. We hope she'll be a family dog. I do my share of looking after her too.

My parents are concerned about me. They send endless pleading texts asking, 'What's the matter? If you don't tell us, we can't help you.' They tell me they are finding it difficult to know what to do, that unless I speak to them and explain why I have withdrawn from family and friends, they are at a loss. I sense their frustration, their exasperation. But the fact is, I cannot explain what is wrong with me either.

My parents decide I must still be mourning Tilly. In fact it is an amalgam of things – which become in my mind like a deafening cacophony of dissonant sounds – that starts the downward spiral.

In the closing months of 2017, my relationship with Donna ends. We've been together almost five years, on and off, and, like the rest of my close friends and family, she does not understand why I have become so remote and withdrawn. But encouraged by her, I agree to take a make-or-break trip to Sweden with her.

Our relationship is a casualty of the catastrophic decline in my mental health, I now realise, but I am also convinced that Ella feels confirmed in her early instincts about us. Her reticence continues and she still senses – lovely though Donna is – that we aren't quite the right match.

Donna's Lhasa Apso, Molly, might well have concluded this too. Our two dogs sustain their uneasy relationship, only just tolerating each other. Ella, who usually bounds enthusiastically into any new house, will stand hesitantly on the doorstep at Donna's. Molly, in turn, is very territorial. If Ella ventures too near to her bed, she growls at her. They have never become buddies.

Donna is kind, sympathetic, but while we are away together, my mind is in turmoil. I'm not in a fit state to make a life-changing decision, but we drift towards the conclusion that we'll go our separate ways. When we return to England, we say regretful goodbyes and resolve to stay friends.

Back at home, I can't switch off the awful clamour in my mind. I feel I'm on a perpetual helter-skelter ride and I can't get off.

I am angry. With everyone and everything. And restlessness leaves me in a constant state of agitation and anxiety. The insomnia is dizzying. It feels as if ten different radio stations are competing for airtime in my head, the din ceaseless and exhausting.

During the day, I drag myself up and go to work, then just stare with glazed eyes at my computer screen, willing the hours to tick by so I can drive home again.

I can't respond to the simplest message, so I don't open my emails. I can't communicate even with those I love best, my family and close friends.

Their anxious texts grow more insistent by the day, yet I cannot muster the energy even to read them. I know how much my parents and my sisters love me and are desperate to help me. But their messages go unanswered as I sink into a mire of despair.

The fact is, I don't believe anyone can reach me, so steep is the downward spiral of my descent.

Concerned friends knock at my door and I look out, shrink back, don't respond.

I know my parents are challenged by my behaviour. They do not know what is happening to me. They cannot grasp the depth or bleakness of it. They wonder why I can't pull myself together and just snap out of it.

I am grateful to Catherine and William, whose work in the field of mental health has given them valuable knowledge and understanding. My parents rely on them, and Pippa, to try to breach the impenetrable wall of my silence.

Sometimes they do break through. My sisters gently cajole me out of the flat now and again. I go to see them for a change of scene. And fleetingly I do feel better. But the relief is temporary. Somehow these transitory moments of happiness make the lows even more crushing.

All colour and emotion has drained from my life. Everything is grey: monochrome and monotone. I write a lot, letters to Ella telling her about the turmoil in my head. I feel somehow guilty, knowing how richly blessed and privileged I am, to be so beset by this awful, debilitating bleakness. But I know too that no amount of money or advantage inures you to it.

It is tricky to describe the condition. It is not merely sadness. It is an illness, a cancer of the mind. It's not a feeling but an absence of feelings. You exist without purpose or direction. I can't feel pleasure or excitement; nothing thrills me or even gives me a sense of anticipation.

Only heart-thudding anxiety – a feeling like someone screaming in my face – propels me out of bed in the morning.

I also feel misunderstood; a complete failure. I wouldn't wish the sense of worthlessness and desperation, the isolation and loneliness on my worst enemy. I think I'm going crazy.

A year passes – the whole of 2017 – in this fog of anxiety and inertia. I barely function, stop talking to my friends, go through the motions of living and working but achieve nothing at all. I come very close to shutting my company down. And my heart is thudding as if it is straining to leap out of my body.

Meanwhile my family, worried to distraction, cannot break through the barrier of my silence.

At night I go to bed, close my eyes, try to suppress the thoughts that are crowding in on me, but they rush in and chase away sleep. My mind is in constant turmoil.

The only respite I have from this noise in my head is when I'm driving. I have an old CD of Stephen Fry reading *Harry Potter*. It takes me back; there is something of my childhood in its boarding school setting and it is a small source of comfort.

I continue to write down my thoughts, as if this will expel them from my mind. It becomes an obsession, this writing. I carry around a satchel containing my laptop and a red folder full of the documents I've amassed. All my notes. Writing is like a nervous tic. I cannot stop.

When I manage to make it to meetings for work, I am physically present but mentally absent. Often I leave the room – without notice or warning – and feel compelled to write down what I am thinking. My mind constantly wanders. I start to consider how I can end my life. Walking in front of a train might be quickest. Or disappearing into remote woodland and cutting my wrists.

These suicidal thoughts possess me. In a room full of people chatting, my mind will wander over the possibilities until someone looks at me and asks, 'James, are you okay?' at which point I make some excuse and say, 'I have to go'.

Then I find myself walking aimlessly, not knowing why I've left or where I am going. All I know is I have to get out of the room.

It is happening more and more frequently. I can be anywhere. At a birthday gathering or a board meeting for Boomf. There is no place I can escape the din in my head.

Running still helps me, and some weekends I set off and find that inadvertently I have run a whole marathon. I'm running away from myself, from my problems. I start to look scrawny. I'm not eating properly. Mum is concerned, but I can't acknowledge that I have a problem that's consuming me. I try to reassure her that I'm just keeping myself healthy.

I continue to write down my jumbled thoughts and keep them in the red folder in my satchel.

One day, stupidly, I leave my laptop and the satchel on the back seat of my car, which I park in Old Church Street. As I put my key in the communal front door, I hear a moped approaching quickly, then the strident blare of a car alarm.

Suspecting something amiss, I open the front door, leaving the dogs in the little shared hallway that leads upstairs to the door of our third-floor flat, and rush back to the car.

As the front door slams behind me, I run into the road to see the moped driver speeding off towards the Embankment, the back window of my car shattered and my computer and bag missing.

It's strange that I'm not worried about the theft of my laptop so much as the reams of notes. I'm frantic. What if the thief discovers the jottings are mine and decides to publish my darkest thoughts about ending my life?

I ring the police and try to explain that it is really important for me to retrieve the stolen folder. The operator tells me calmly that an officer will be assigned to my case. I'm given a crime number.

It is hard to describe the disproportionate distress I feel. I'm wrangling with the bleakest thoughts imaginable and still even my closest family don't know the extent or scope of them. I have not even begun to understand myself what is going on in my head.

And now a thief has access to my innermost thoughts. My fevered mind conjures up all kinds of newspaper headlines about Catherine's brother wanting to take his own life.

But there are more pressing practical problems to deal with. I realise that in my haste to nab the thief, I've left my house keys inside the front door and have locked myself out. Fortunately, my downstairs neighbour is just coming back from playing tennis. She lets me into the hallway, where the dogs, confused and agitated by my sudden departure, are waiting.

My neighbour can see how stressed I am. She sits me down, makes me a cup of tea and asks kindly, 'Is everything all right, James?'

'I'm fine,' I bluff. 'It's just that all my work's been stolen.'

Over the next days I can't stop thinking about all the painfully personal thoughts I've documented. It becomes an irrational obsession to try to replicate them. I scribble continually. And I worry endlessly about whose hands those words are now in.

Then I get a phone call. Unidentified caller. Normally I'm paranoid about answering calls from people I don't know, worried that it could be a journalist asking about Donna, but this time, for some unaccountable reason, I pick up.

'Kensington and Chelsea Police,' a voice says. 'Your bag's been found under a hedge, but your laptop's been taken.'

I'm unconcerned about the stolen laptop, only interested in my papers. 'Please let me know if there's a red folder in the bag,' I implore, seeing a spark of hope.

'We'll collect it first and see if there are any fingerprints on it,' the police officer tells me evenly.

Later that day, another call from the police: 'By the way, there is a red folder full of papers in your bag.'

I feel a huge wave of relief: thank God I'll get my scribblings back.

I start to recognise the paradox of my mental state. Although I have so many people around me who love me and want to support me, I feel utterly alone. And I can't understand why.

Then everything reaches a climax. I drive to work, arrive at the office car park and switch off the engine. But I can't get out of the car. I can't even find the impetus to open the door. I unclip my seat belt. Sit there. Sit there. Someone wheels a pallet outside and spots me. The last thing I want is a concerned voice asking if I'm okay. I pretend to be on the phone, put my hand up in a 'please wait a minute' gesture.

But can I get out of the car later?

I can't.

I know now I have no option. I have to call our family doctor.

I've already consulted her once. At the end of 2016, when my heart started beating so fast it felt like an engine revving at full tilt, I knew something was wrong, so I phoned her and had tests that revealed arrhythmia – problems with the rhythm of my heart – caused by stress and anxiety.

After a short time on medication, the symptoms subsided. But against doctor's advice, I did nothing about treating the root cause of the problem.

But now I accept I must call her again. I ring her from the car as I sit there unable to move.

She doesn't answer, but a text message pings back. 'All okay?'

'No, not really,' I text back.

It is the first time I've admitted the truth. I'm not all right.

A moment later, my phone rings. 'James, where are you? Do you want to talk?'

I feel as if I'm trying to hold in a waterfall of emotion. I struggle to get the words out. I'm close to tears.

'I'm at work. Sitting in the car. I'm not okay. I need some help,' I manage to say.

'Do you want to come here?'

But I can't move. And I say as much.

'It's really important that you try to speak to someone. I'll call you in an hour. Meanwhile I'll see if I can get an appointment for you,' she says.

I turn the car round and drive back to London. Ella, who is sitting on the passenger seat, looks confused. She knows we usually go to the office, but today we're going straight home.

She always sits with her head against the gearstick so that every time I change gear she gets an ear rub. She nestles in closer next to me, sensing that all is not right.

Back at the flat, I pace up and down, round and round. Senselessly, without purpose. Ella just sits quietly watching me from the middle of the room. I walk into the kitchen, put the kettle on. Several times I go back, repeat the futile exercise, never making a cup of tea.

The phone rings. Our doctor again. 'James, I've spoken to a psychologist who can fit you in for an appointment tomorrow. Would that be okay?'

I agree to go at 10 a.m. the next day. Wimpole Street. The relief of admitting I need help gives me a brief respite from the perpetual night wakefulness. I sleep. But next morning, I go grudgingly. Ella is not with me – I don't know if she'll be welcome – and her absence sets me on edge.

At the surgery, I mutter and mumble, can't look the receptionist in the eye. It seems a shaming admission that I need help with my mental health.

Impatient to get better, I expect an instant diagnosis. A miracle cure. But I come out of the appointment feeling even worse, because nothing has been resolved. I'm almost angry. Why doesn't the pain stop? Why haven't I got a prescription to make me better?

I ring our doctor. 'It hasn't worked,' I say flatly. 'I just feel as if we didn't connect.'

'I understand, James,' she replies. 'I think I know someone who will be better suited to you.'

Chapter Seven

A Spark of Light in the Darkness

Reluctantly I agree to take my doctor's advice and see consultant psychiatrist Dr Stephen Pereira.

But I'm impatient to get myself fixed, irrationally annoyed when his secretary says there is a four-day wait. I'm close to the edge. It feels too long.

I don't sleep for four days and nights. I pace the flat restlessly. Pippa comes over, but I double-lock the front door and refuse to let her in. I want to stay in my own space, detached from everyone, until I am mended.

In my head it still feels as if a thousand radio stations are competing to tune themselves in. The din is dizzying. I'm wrung out, sleepless, exhausted.

I do not cry. I have cried so much over the past months that I'm dry of tears. There are none left. I've lost the capacity to express emotion.

There is no point in anything any more. I give up. I've lost every ounce of will to fight. The black mood is taking over. I just want this darkness to lift. Otherwise I have no desire to go on living.

Only Ella gives me the courage to fight the dark thoughts that I see as Dementors. They are the product of J. K. Rowling's fertile imagination: 'the foulest creatures that walk this earth . . . Get too near a Dementor and every good feeling, every happy memory will be sucked out of you . . . You'll be left with nothing,' she writes in *Harry Potter and the Prisoner of Azkaban*.

And this is exactly how I feel: as if Dementors have sucked the joy out of me, leaving an empty husk. To dispel them you have to think of something positive. My dogs, and Ella in particular, are my sole source of happiness, my reason to keep going.

They give me the courage to face life; their very existence is a balm to my hurt mind. They need me to look after them. With Ella I feel a special empathy. Actually, I think it is she who is looking after me.

Just feeding and walking her gives me a brief respite from the clamour in my mind. These simple daily tasks keep me from complete despair. I realise, through the fog of those days, that I need to stay alive for her.

My appointment with Dr Pereira is at Borough Market, a bus and two Tube rides then a short walk away. Ella is with me. I'm almost willing the doctor to tell me she can't come in to the appointment with me so that I have a reason to back out of it.

I feel ambivalent: I am desperate to be well, but I think I'm beyond saving. I don't know how anyone can reach me.

The journey there is a slow form of torture. But Ella, always at my side, senses every nuance of my mood. She knows how vital her role is. She knows she is needed to provide support.

She has a habit of nudging my hand, enticing me to stroke her head. If I remove my hand, she gently prods me until I put it back. I am sure this is her way of comforting me. It's as if she's holding my hand.

She is the reason that I dare to leave the flat and brave the troubling bustle of London in the first place. As I make the journey, I feel fearful, as if the world is staring at me. But Ella graciously deflects attention away from me and towards herself. She is a courteous dog. She does not bound heedlessly up to strangers, but quietly assesses whether they want to befriend her.

If they show interest in her, she looks to me for permission first, then obliges with gentle affection, offering her head to be patted.

She walks with me through Borough Market, sniffing the unfamiliar food smells, picking up morsels that have fallen on the ground. I manage to smile to myself: at least one of us is having a nice time.

I'm still hoping Ella will be my excuse not to go in. I ring the buzzer, and a receptionist greets me with a huge smile. 'Ah, who's this?' she asks me, stroking Ella. Immediately I am comforted, disarmed. I forget why I am there and start chatting about dogs.

Ten minutes on, the receptionist, so engrossed in our conversation, has forgotten to let Dr Pereira know I'm there. He comes out to see if I've arrived. 'Do you mind if I bring Ella in with me?' I ask. To my surprise, he says: 'She's more than welcome.'

Ella coaxes me through the door. Irrationally, I still feel residual anger. Will the doctor even listen to me? How can he help me when he knows nothing about the complex machinations of my brain?

I don't realise that the process is slow and painstaking. It will be years before my tortured mind starts to heal.

I sit down. Ella has a sniff around the room, then parks her head in my lap. Instinctively I give her a little rub behind her ears, and as I start talking, her eyes close contentedly.

Dr Pereira asks me to start at the beginning, to go back to my earliest memory. 'Here we go,' I think, the words unvoiced. 'The problem is here and now. Let's fix it and move on.'

But Ella is happy and it is a comfort to me to have her alongside me. With my hand on her head, I feel soothed. She is the conduit for my thoughts, the link that helps me communicate. I feel a calming sensation flood through me. My resistance to talking recedes.

My first conversation with Dr Pereira, far from being fraught and angry, feels like a relief. But two hours later, I am drained, tripping over my words.

'I want to know what's wrong with me,' I say. 'What is the solution? Please give me a prescription and I'll be on my way.' I'm still frustrated, confused and mildly irritated by the apparent irrelevance of his questions.

'We have to try to unravel why you feel as you do. It isn't going to be a quick fix,' he tells me.

That isn't what I want to hear. I want reassurance that everything is fine, that if I go away and collect some tablets, I'll feel better in a matter of days.

But there is no such comfort. Instead, Dr Pereira asks me to book another appointment in a week.

'Can you bring Ella along with you to the next session?' he asks, realising the soothing effect she has on me.

And that is a solace. Ella is welcome. Actually, she is invited. I know that next time will be easier.

On the way home, I make time for a little treat for her, a snack at Borough Market. Dear Ella, my friend in need, my salvation.

There is, it emerges, much more talking to do. And the next time, when the words start to flow, they are constructive, thoughtful.

I begin to realise that my childhood shaped me into the person I am today, that events I initially dismissed as irrelevant all, in fact, have their own significance. At Dr Pereira's request I bring in old school reports.

We even talk about the fact that I am left-handed, yet I struggled as a young boy to conform with my classmates and wrote with my right hand, which impeded me and made me even slower.

I also deliberately made my handwriting illegible to cover up for the fact that I could not spell. Although I have now embraced the fact that I am left-handed, I still write indecipherable scribble to mask my poor spelling.

I start to speak openly, and feel hopeful that with Ella helping me and Dr Pereira untangling the chaotic jumble of my thoughts, I will make some progress.

But there is a physical aspect of this malaise of the mind, too. At night, when I lie sleepless and restless, I feel my heart pounding in my chest, a frenzied drumbeat that makes me feel as if it will burst from my ribcage.

I lie there, fearing that my distress is so palpable it will rouse Ella, and then I glance across at her and she is already awake, looking at me intently as if to say, 'What's wrong?'

I have an app that takes my pulse. It pounds as if I'm running fit to burst my lungs. It flutters and stalls. I check Ella's pulse – a steady rhythmic beat – and know something is wrong with mine.

I mention the racing, stuttering pulse to Dr Pereira when I see him next. Immediately he refers me to my GP, who in turn books me in with a cardiologist. He checks my pulse and diagnoses atrial fibrillation, which can, if untreated, lead to a stroke.

I go to hospital for tests and scans. My heart rate is monitored by an ECG. I'm put on medication to control my irregular heartbeat, which I take to this day.

I'm acutely aware of how my mental health has impacted on the physical: my mental torment is reflected in the frantic beating of my heart.

After more sessions with Dr Pereira, he tells me: 'James, I believe you have clinical depression. There are lots of different layers to unpick and we can put them into categories and start working on them.'

Once I start to talk, it becomes easier. Then he throws me a massive curveball. 'I'm starting to think you might also have attention deficit disorder.'

I laugh. It is the first time I've laughed in a long time. For years I've felt misunderstood, that no one quite gets me. Perhaps this is the reason.

Through these meetings with Dr Pereira, I learn that depression is only a small part of the complex jigsaw that is me.

There are more sessions and I find that talking helps. Every meeting gives me enough courage to go to the next one.

And when I am diagnosed with ADD, all the quirks and foibles of my character start to make sense.

ADD, an adult variant of attention deficit hyperactivity disorder – which is associated with disruptive children – produces a range of symptoms, some of which are like autism. And when I'm told I have it, it is a revelation. It explains so much.

It is the reason I have trouble focusing, why my mind wanders off into extravagant daydreams, why simple tasks like making my bed assume the same enormity as filing my tax return.

It explains the convoluted journey my mind takes when I'm faced with a very simple exercise like writing a thank-you letter. I believe so strongly in saying thank you, and in my mind I know what I want to write, but I can't translate my thoughts into physical actions.

I think: 'I want to send a jar of honey with the letter but I can't find the person's postcode,' so although it would take only 30 seconds to text them and ask for it, I'm thinking, 'I must also find that article they'd like to read' and 'I want to invite them to dinner, but they've just broken up with their girlfriend/boyfriend and I don't know if it's the right time.' So instead of writing, I do nothing.

Now that I'm telling you about it, it seems ludicrous, doesn't it? I even laugh at myself.

ADD explains why I'm restless, energetic and impulsive; why I start tasks but can't complete them; why sometimes I seem impatient and don't listen because my mind is galloping off on some flight of fancy.

However, I also see it as a gift: it accounts for my creativity and emotional intensity. It means that I come up with fantastically original ideas – but it also explains why I have had difficulties with the minutiae of running a business.

And yet I've always run my own businesses, because I couldn't have coped with the constraints and routine of being employed, and it's hard work. Even without ADD and dyslexia it's like pushing water uphill. The fact that I suffer from both – and now this black depression – explains why I have not been able to cope, why self-doubt erodes my confidence.

ADD. Clinical depression. The two conditions explain such a lot about me.

Dr Pereira wants to send me to a cognitive behavioural therapist. I resist. It feels like a waste of time. How can talking cure me? I tell my GP: 'It's not working. All I do is talk, and no one is really listening.'

'James, it's a process,' she tells me. 'If you'd broken your arm, it wouldn't be fixed immediately. You'd have a diagnosis, repair and rehab. Try to see it like that: an illness. You have to give yourself time to heal.'

So I continue, because everyone says I should. And Ella, of course, comes with me, which makes it bearable. But still it feels a dauntingly long task. Three, six, twelve months, and my attention span is short. Still, I cannot let my mind wander, because it will go into dark places.

I keep on talking until I feel drained. Dr Pereira says little, but he is listening keenly, assessing me.

He wants me to learn more about ADD, and he gives me a book, *The Gift of Adult ADD: How to Transform Your Challenges and Build on Your Strengths* by Lara Honos-Webb.

'Highlight the bits that apply to you,' he says – and I do. By the time I've read it, I've highlighted the whole book in green and orange. It is as if the entire thing has been written just for me. A window into my complex mind. It *all* applies to me.

The knowledge that others feel exactly as I do – that this is a recognised condition – cheers me. I don't feel so isolated. It makes me trust the healing process more. In fact, I am so comforted by the book that I buy copies for all the family: Mum and Dad, Catherine and William, Pippa and James.

It is the first chink of light, the start of letting them in on the dark tumult in my mind. But I still haven't opened up to them completely. I have not yet given Dr Pereira permission to talk to them about my mental condition.

Even so, I hope the book will help their understanding of me. Certainly it helps me know why I start every job thinking I am doomed to fail; why I've never learned to follow instructions; why some people write me off as lazy, stupid, a mess.

A bit of me wonders if the undiagnosed ADD was a trigger for my clinical depression. In everything from relationships to work I felt like a square peg in a round hole. That's why I spiralled into negativity, why I approached everything with a profound sense of my own inadequacies.

Looking back on my childhood and adolescence now, it all starts to make sense.

I recall my school reports: 'James would be very good at chemistry if only he applied himself.' It's true. I loved chemistry. I found it fascinating. But my mind had to go on that circuitous journey to get to the answer that everyone else found immediately.

It was as if my brain was wired differently. I was always enthusiastic, but – and there was always a 'but' – in everything from music to sport I was no good at taking instructions.

It wasn't that I was rebellious, just that I had to find my own way of understanding things.

And all the time I was compensating for failing to know what was going on. It was exhausting, this continual pretence that I was coping, understanding. And it has dogged me through school, university and into my adult life.

Bit by bit, almost despite myself, I start to enjoy the CBT sessions.

They are useful because they are pragmatic: they help me identify my problems and solve them. They give me the armoury to cope. I have goals to achieve, solutions to current problems. I cannot wait to get out into the world and use these new tools.

CBT builds my confidence and mental strength. I look back on the things I felt incapable of achieving – because I was scared of my incompetence – and feel new vigour to take on these tasks.

It teaches me a valuable lesson: that vulnerability is not a weakness. Vulnerability allows us to ask questions; it permits us to admit, too, that there are some things we cannot do.

Vitally, it also teaches me to finish the many tasks that used to be strewn, half completed, in my wake.

Armed with an enormous A2 notepad – I know I'll have difficulty losing an item this big – I write in marker pen, in large letters, the jobs I aim to complete. I do not turn the page until the tasks are done, and when they are, I take enormous satisfaction in ticking them off, one by one.

Before I started CBT, I would accumulate piles of Christmas and birthday cards to friends and relatives. These would languish forgotten in drawers for years, simply because although I would get as far as writing the greeting inside, and even the address on the envelope, and buying and sticking on the stamps, I'd fall short at the final hurdle and wouldn't take them to the postbox.

Now letters and cards make their way to the intended recipients, and I feel such a sense of achievement.

I can see how my lack of self-belief led inexorably to depression. And there were lessons for everyone as – later on in my recovery – my family got involved and realised that my mental health problems had their roots in my childhood.

It is often the case that your family, who love and know you best, are also the most critical of you. It accounted for the impasse: why Mum and Dad found it difficult to talk to me about my mental health, because they felt they knew me better than I did. I in turn resisted their help.

Their intentions were kind. They were hugely supportive. But some of their suggestions were not actually constructive. They were resistant to therapy. And their biggest worry was that I would become dependent on antidepressants.

I, in turn, was defensive, annoyed. I'd already made up my mind that I didn't want to take prescription drugs for my depression. I felt that would be sweeping the problem under the carpet, merely tamping down the feelings I should be addressing, and my parents' involvement felt like needless interference.

Although I was making strides in the right direction – and finally I'd begun tentatively to broach the subject of my illness with Mum and Dad – my mental health was still fragile.

Christmas 2017 was approaching and the whole family were going to Glen Affric, the estate in the Scottish Highlands owned by Pippa's husband's family. Frankly, I didn't want to go. I was still sleeping badly, my recovery in its tentative early stages.

I'd been prescribed sleeping pills, a temporary measure to help the insomnia so I could get some rest, and my parents were worried about them as they had been about the thought of antidepressants. It didn't help that they had no idea about the slow process of disentanglement my chaotic mind was going through. I was still very much a closed book.

Actually, although I was taking small steps forward, my parents thought I was getting worse. Because I was quietly processing everything I'd talked about with Dr Pereira, they thought that I'd become even more introverted. To the outside world it probably looked that way, and it was, I can now see, very worrying for them.

They were uncomfortable with the fact that I'd been labelled 'clinically depressed'. To people of their generation I can understand why it was concerning. Society was only just starting to break through the stigma.

Catherine and Pippa understood, though, because they had been exposed to similar experiences through friends who'd had depression, and they helped to convey what was going on to our parents.

But as our family planned their jolly Highland Christmas, I was still adamant: I would stay at home on my own with Ella and hide.

Mum was so worried that she corralled the whole family into sending me cheery invitations. Up popped one from my aunt and uncle. 'There's always a bed for you here,' they offered hopefully. My cousins sent similar messages.

It was exactly what I did not want. Enforced cheerfulness, noise, laughter. I felt mentally and physically wrung out, tired of talking and thinking. The last thing I wanted was to pretend to be happy.

Meanwhile I'd had a board meeting with the newly appointed Boomf CEO and fellow directors. They were aware of my fragile state of mind; how could they fail to be? The evidence was there in my detachment, the unfocused inertia, the inability to accomplish even the most prosaic of tasks.

But still I felt the weight of my responsibilities. I was loath to take time off. During that meeting, though, they were insistent: 'We want you back at work, but not like this.'

I'd been scared to tell them I had clinical depression. I thought they'd spurn me, that deals would fall through, that I was hindering the business. I saw myself as a risk.

But they assured me it wasn't so. I was so fortunate they were encouraging and supportive, which meant I was signed off on extended leave from work. Ultimately I never went back to the company.

So having stood down, I woke on Monday morning and thought, 'What am I going to do with all this time?' I'd been going through the motions: driving to work, sitting at my desk, watching the clock tick sluggishly through the day until it was time to drive home.

I'd pace round the flat, restive, unsettled, and attempt to cook something. But my appetite had deserted me. I didn't want to eat. I was not remotely hungry. The weight fell off me. I lost a stone and a half during this time.

Every time I tried to force myself to eat, I'd feel sick. Anxiety was literally choking me. If I did manage to swallow a mouthful, minutes later I'd retch.

In these interminable days I spent alone, the darkest of thoughts would crowd in on me again . . . Until one morning Ella again came to my rescue.

She often greets me with a shoe in her mouth, encouragement to come out for a walk, but her salutation today is subtly different. She is carrying one of my hiking boots, the stout ones I wear for serious treks in the mountains.

She has picked it up, but it is heavy and she cannot quite make it to my feet. So she drops it in the middle of the room. Despite myself, I laugh. And I see her sweet gesture of support as a sign. We need time away together, just the dogs and me.

So the next morning at 4 a.m., when usually I would lie sleepless, I get up and leave for my beloved Lake District, revelling in the four-and-a-half-hour drive in the company of my dogs, with the magical *Harry Potter* audiobook as our soundtrack.

I think back to my childhood, to the first edition my grandmother bought me; then to the ordeal of school homework, when I was told to read six chapters, which seemed an insurmountable hurdle. How wonderful it would have been if I'd been able to listen to the audiobook then!

As I drive north through the grey light of that December dawn, warnings of an incoming storm fail to deter me. In fact I think of it as a good omen: less likely that I'll see a soul on my trip. I actually feel a lightening of my heart.

I reach the primitive cottage that will be our home for the next few days. There is no electricity, no mobile phone reception. I can stay there unhindered by unwelcome intrusions from the outside world.

I feel this elemental need to get back to basics, to strip away everything extraneous from my life, and here is the place to do it, in a cottage with no running water, where the sole source of heat is a back boiler served by an open fire.

So my day-to-day challenges will be simple ones: fetching water from the stream, keeping the cottage warm, settling the dogs by a cosy fire, feeding us all. I've brought basic supplies: tinned steak and kidney pie, packet soups; nothing gourmet. But to me it is the food of love, and bit by bit my appetite is returning.

Outside, storm clouds lour over the valley below, but on the mountaintops there is snow. I get myself set up. Walk the dogs, chop wood, light a fire; settle Ella and her daughters, Luna and Inka, by the roaring flames, watch the steam rise from their damp coats. And there in the comforting fug of heat in that tiny, basic room, I feel a few short seconds of what I can only describe as happiness.

The respite from the turmoil in my mind lasts, perhaps, 20 seconds. Less than half a minute. But it gives me hope that perhaps next time it will be longer. Perhaps there will be a minute's reprieve from the darkness. I can build on that, one tiny step at a time.

It has been a long day. I fall asleep in a chair by the fire, only to be woken by the cold at 2 a.m. The fire has burned down to embers. Inka jumps onto my lap for a cuddle. Half sleepwalking, I stumble upstairs and curl up in my cold sleeping bag, and for the first time in years, I fall into a deep, dreamless sleep.

The next day I wake to clear skies – the storm has passed overnight – and the lure of the snow-capped mountains.

I prepare for the day ahead: stir the fire into life, heat chicken soup, pour it into a Thermos, pack it into my rucksack with cheese treats for the dogs and a flapjack. I have a walk in mind, and it is one of the old Wainwright routes, familiar to me from his pocket guides of the Lakeland Fells. 'Right,' I tell the dogs, 'we're off.'

A dusting of snow covers the Old Man of Coniston; the air is crisp, glacial, the winter sun a harbinger of hope. As I climb this Lakeland peak I've known since boyhood, I feel a sense that life is seeping like spring sap through my veins.

Only the previous day, I was in London, my life crumbling around me; now my mind feels freer, as if the shackles are slowly breaking.

Ella is at my side, with Luna and Inka bounding ahead, their spaniel ears hung with icicles. Ella is always closest to me. She has slept on my bed, my constant companion, since she was a pup. She registers every flicker of my mood, and today she senses the pall of cloud lifting. She revels in my new buoyancy. Everything is going to be all right.

For the first time in years, I feel myself coming to life again. I bound along the path, Ella skittering by my side, then darting ahead between cairns and rocky outcrops before pausing to wait for me to catch up.

The wide sky is cerulean blue; snow crunches underfoot. I feel a slow smile creep across my face. It is the sense of freedom that cheers me, and I don't know who is enjoying this most, Ella or me. My senses tingle with the thrill of it. Colour is filtering back into my world. I'm alert once more to the beauty of the pine-clad slopes that descend to glassy Coniston Water; to the open sky, the majesty of the mountains.

The silence is healing. I'm glad to be here with my most loyal companion, taking in the Lakeland view that has been familiar since my earliest memories.

Ella knows the place too, from when I first brought her here as a puppy, almost 13 years ago, and carried her up this very path in my backpack, just as my father had carried me. It is hard to believe that she has spent so many years at my side, my ever-present shadow; an extension of me.

I talk to her all the way, as I often do. 'How lucky are we?' I say, a question I wouldn't have imagined myself asking a year ago. Her eloquent brown eyes seem to speak to me. She agrees. We are both so fortunate.

What I do not realise is that, given my fragile mental state, my unexplained absence from London has created huge concern. My silent phone is pinging with messages, a bombardment from my worried family and friends. 'Where are you, James?' 'What's going on?' 'Are you okay?' I'm out of range, completely oblivious to the barrage.

I am absorbed in the walk, but stop to wonder if I should continue on the treacherous icy path ahead. Common sense says I should go back. But my mind is in a fighting phase. It tells me I must accomplish something.

So although it is not a sensible decision, I continue. The path becomes more hazardous. The dogs' paws struggle to find grip. A slippery ice sheet looms ahead. One by one I pick up the dogs and carry them to safety across it on my shoulders.

I tell them that if we reach the summit, there will be a reward of cheese. I am even quietly reprimanding myself: 'James, turn back. This is dangerous.' My biggest fear is not for my own safety but putting the dogs in danger. I do not want to be reckless with their precious lives. I am the leader of their pack, the head of the team guiding them up a mountain. Should I be taking such risks?

And then, before I even realise it, we have reached the summit. The view stretches across to the higher peak of Helvellyn. I pause to drink in the sheer glory of it.

I've known these mountains all my life, but I've rarely climbed them in the snow, and now the unalloyed joy of being alive grips me. I feel as if I am standing on the apex of the world, and the thrill is so dizzying I start to yell.

'Ah-hahhh!' I shout. 'Hello!' (Nothing comes back but a distant baa from a Herdwick sheep.) I am embarrassed by the noise I make, but it is liberating. I cry, 'Thank you!' to the mountains, as if this walk has been made just for me.

It feels as if I am flushing out all the toxins that have poisoned my mind. There are tears in my eyes, and every emotion I've felt over the past bleak years – anger, anxiety, dread, fear – floods out of me. A purging.

I pour my chicken broth and sip it, thinking it is the best soup I have ever tasted. The dogs devour their cheese treats. We all share the flapjack. And it is like an epiphany, as if the world is saying to me, 'Welcome back, James.'

Here it is again: this ray of light in the darkness of my mind, piercing remorselessly through the gloom. And in this glorious moment at the peak of the mountain – in this glimpse of hope – I think: 'It is worth staying alive just for this. This is pure happiness.'

Happiness. It is nothing complicated or costly, just the act of walking on a cold, crisp winter's day, in fresh air and silence, with my dogs for company. There is struggle there, too, and challenge accomplished. All this contributes to the sense of fulfilment I feel.

I like analogies. It has been an uphill battle, but I've reached the top and now I'm on the homeward path. My mood is so buoyant I almost skip. And the dogs are bounding too, loping along the snowy descent, sure-footed as mountain goats.

On the way, we pass a rock pool in a stream that feeds the Lakes. Its edges are iced to the bank. Usually I wait until August before I swim in this beck. It's a long-held ritual. But today I say to Ella – almost joking – 'Shall we have a swim?'

And then I answer myself: 'Why not?' So I strip off, break the ice and jump in, Ella then Inka and Luna following, evidently thinking I'm crazy.

The cold is numbing, literally breathtaking. Every nerve end and sinew tingles into life with the startling chill of it. And as I duck my head under the water, I shiver and laugh. The sound is unfamiliar to me; it feels as if it comes from someone else. I have not felt the endorphin rush of such elation for so long. I have not embraced the rapture of it.

But it is, it seems, another part of the ritual of cleansing the toxins from my mind.

The dogs paddle with their noses above the surface, and I strike out into the freezing depths for just a few metres before swimming back to the water's edge.

I have not packed a towel, so, knowing there is no one to see, I run round in circles, do star jumps and shake myself dry like the dogs.

We're all shaking ourselves on the bank when a rainstorm of shivering droplets comes over. I've never felt more exultant. It's a curious truth, but I feel I want to be a dog, to just live in the here and now, to get away from the pressures and obligations of life.

My teeth are chattering, my fingers are numb and I can barely tie my bootlaces, which have stiffened in the frosty air. But there is something exhilarating in the warmth that slowly pulses through my freezing body.

My blood is thrumming as I run up the hill to our old stone shepherd's hut. And I feel like a child again: free, wild, unfettered.

Back at the cottage – this unspoiled place that has not changed, in its slow, perennial pace, for centuries – I am still tingling with cold. The dogs shiver, yearning for the warmth of a log fire.

As we're off-grid, I light the Tilley lamps, then collect water in pans from the beck and make a wood fire to heat it on top of the back boiler.

I feel a growing sense of pleasure at this simple toil. There is something about the slow pace of collecting kindling and chopping wood that helps heal a troubled mind. You cannot rush the tasks. You work at a pace that has not changed for millennia.

When the boiler is lit, I heat pans of water for the hip bath, then soap myself in the steaming heat of it.

Afterwards, I feed the fire with more logs. And as a warming glow fills the room, I pour myself a whisky mac and think: 'This perfect day was made just for me.'

I make a haphazard cheese fondue from scraps of Cheddar, Stilton and Babybel, thickening it with flour, adding a splash of white wine, and it is the best thing I have ever tasted.

I look at my little dog family, curled on their beds in the flickering warmth, steam rising from the glossy nap of their coats.

Contented. That is the word for my current state of mind. And I know that Ella, above all my dogs – the wise old lady of my little brood – feels my new-found happiness as acutely as any human could do.

Chapter Eight

A Christmas Epiphany

———

For much of the next day, I sleep: you cannot overestimate its restorative power.

I've been away for two and a half days, but I have to get back to London for an appointment with Dr Pereira. I do not want to miss it. I know I am not yet healed – and the therapy is doing me good.

We set out, the dogs and I, on our southbound journey. I know the exact spot where the mobile phone signal comes back. As we reach it, the pings come thick and fast, the messages from home getting ever more frantic. 'Where are you, James?' 'We're desperate to get hold of you.' 'Okay, we're really worried now.'

My family thought I had gone away to die, to end my own life. I realise that now. I feel contrite; full of regret for not recognising just how panicked I'd made them.

At the time, however, irrationally – and unjustifiably – I feel annoyed, controlled. I'm a grown man. I've been away for a few days and it has been the most formative trip of my life. Actually, I didn't go away to end my life; I went to find a reason to live. And I discovered it.

So why is everyone intruding on my decision?

I fill up with fuel and decide not to call anyone, knowing they'll have seen the blue WhatsApp ticks signalling that I've read their messages and am therefore alive. Then I pick up a voicemail from Pippa: 'James, we're all so worried about you. Where on earth are you?' Her voice is tearful with concern, with just an edge of reprimand.

I message her back, trying to quell my irritation: 'I've just been to the Lake District for a couple of days. Do I have to seek your permission?'

I spend the rest of the journey feeling a mix of remorse for my irresponsible behaviour, and defiance. I know if I'd told my family I was going away, the trip would not have served its purpose.

They would have felt compelled to come and check on me, and I'd have felt tethered to their concern. I wouldn't have had that wonderful sense of freedom from the worries that threatened to choke me. Actually, I wouldn't have found my reason to live.

I was making progress, but because I'd shut my parents out from the process, my next challenge was to try to explain to them that although they might not yet realise it, therapy was really helping me.

But when I arrived back in London, the rush of euphoria I'd felt in the Lake District receded. The nights were drawing in; I felt a gloom descend. Once more I started avoiding invitations, leaving social events abruptly, walking aimlessly.

Driving became a solace – even a form of therapy, in which my mind would be freed to think – and sometimes I'd jump in the car with Ella, head for a beach and go for a long walk. Once she and I went to Cornwall, just for the day.

On December Sundays I'd go to Chelsea Old Church for Christmas services. I loved the sense of community, the singing of familiar tunes, the comfort of tradition and the aura of peace. For the time I was there, I was answerable to no one.

The vicar, who had not seen me since Catherine and William's wedding, seemed delighted by my return.

But as the final note of the last carol rang out, I'd drop a handful of coins in the collection box and leave smartly. I stayed to join in the singing, but I didn't want to speak to anyone after the service.

And still the thought of a family Christmas in Scotland loomed. Until the very last moment I was certain I wouldn't go. Being there with such a large gathering of family around me would feel claustrophobic, I told myself. I wouldn't be able to get away when I wanted to. I'd feel hemmed in, suffocated.

Then, at the eleventh hour, I changed my mind. I decided I'd go, taking the dogs, of course. They would provide my excuse to leave for long walks whenever I needed to escape into solitude.

Usually we were all impatient for long car journeys to end, but, travelling alone, I was in no rush to arrive at Glen Affric, where Mum and Dad, Pippa and her husband James Matthews, his parents Jane and David and his brother Spencer and wife Vogue had already gathered.

I took a circuitous route, drove slowly; marshalled every tactic to delay my arrival. Actually, I was afraid; worried I'd be overwhelmed, that I'd regress.

Affric Lodge is one of those glorious Victorian houses that feels just right for Christmas. A sturdy, turreted stone mansion on the edge of a tranquil loch, it has views over the Highland Hills, log fires that blaze a welcome, comfy sofas, and sporting scenes by Sir Edwin Landseer festooning the drawing room. But although I knew I was extremely privileged to be invited there, there was no comfort in the opulent surroundings.

I arrived late on 23 December, feeling awkward, just as everyone was sitting down to dinner. They welcomed me warmly; my parents with relief and delight that I'd actually decided to join them. But their efforts at conviviality only made me feel even more ill at ease. Everyone was so palpably treading on eggshells, trying not to upset me. I started to feel the familiar black cloud pressing down on me. The need to get outside consumed me.

When I'd expressed doubts to Dr Pereira about going away with my family, he'd told me: 'Go. It'll do you good. It's everything you love: mountains, fresh air, and you'll have your dogs. If you find it all too much, just go out for a walk with them.'

So next day I escaped to the hills with the dogs. I busied myself with outdoor tasks like collecting wood and bringing in logs. I helped the gamekeepers.

And I plunged into the icy loch, girding myself for the numbing cold. The freezing chill was once again breathtaking. As I ducked my head under the water, I shivered and laughed.

These dips continued to help restore my mental health. It was as if they woke my deadened senses to the joy of life.

And bit by bit, my mood began to lighten. I started to realise – the revelation was a slow-dawning one – just how much my loving and supportive family meant to me. Having them here around me, their faces wreathed in smiles, wanting so desperately to help me, made me feel blessed, not confined.

I realised how I'd mistreated them; I felt bad for not recognising how much they just wanted to help.

In the wake of my epiphany, solitary walks became family walks – although I often extended them and went off on my own when everyone else had turned for home.

On Christmas morning, we woke to find the dark forest frosted white. Snow had fallen overnight. It was a white Christmas, and we crunched through the Caledonian pines – one of the oldest forests in Scotland – marvelling at how each tree had its own character, shaped by the prevailing winds.

Later in the day, Spencer and I walked the Affric Trail, three hours round the loch with its majestic views over one of Scotland's most beautiful glens. Ella was with us, never too far from my side, racing ahead then turning back, eyes watchful, to check my progress.

We stopped at a little fisherman's bothy – a tiny one-room hut, warmed by a log-burning stove – to eat mince pies and drink a slug of whisky from a flask.

By 4 p.m. we were back at Affric Lodge ready for our turkey meal, eaten by candlelight in front of a blazing fire. Then, in the evening, fuelled by whisky and more enthusiasm than aptitude, we tried some Scottish dancing. Despite myself, I enjoyed it and found myself smiling.

And as the festive days passed, my pleasure was genuine. On a day of calm frosts and pale sunlight, I took Ella paddleboarding on a mirror-smooth loch. The colour was once again creeping back into my life. My beloved dog was at my side.

Those rare moments of happiness were starting to coalesce into hours of contentment. I was building my sense of purpose again.

In January comes my first session of the new year with Dr Pereira. I cannot wait to see him again, to continue my progress.

'Would it be sensible to bring my family into the discussions now?' I ask him. He tells me he was about to suggest exactly the same thing.

So we start with my parents. I begin to open up to them, to tell them about the therapy, the problems that began early in my boyhood. They attend two sessions with me but remain bewildered, full of questions I cannot answer. Their prevailing mood is regret. 'If only we'd known how you felt . . .' they say.

I tell them not to reproach themselves. When I was at school, there was no one to diagnose ADD, no resources; scant awareness of it. How could they have known about it?

It takes them some time to grasp the complex machinations of my mind, to get on the right wavelength.

Then Catherine and Pippa come on board, and they understand straight away. They come to a session with me, and the fact that they are here, wanting so much to help me, makes me burst into tears.

I did not tell even Dr Pereira how closely my thoughts had wandered towards suicide. It is he who, with my consent, now talks to my sisters, simply because I find it so hard to articulate what has been going on in my mind. It is the first time they become aware of the extent of my struggles.

They listen and learn. Catherine has already done a lot of work through her mental health initiative Heads Together, and she asks Dr Pereira some pertinent questions. She understands so much. I'm overwhelmed. I feel such gratitude and admiration for her, for her knowledge and compassion.

And my confidence is growing.

Pippa, equally dear to me, wants to help in practical ways, and she suggests I move in with her and James. They have a house in Chelsea, just round the corner from our family's flat in Old Church Street. James is intent on helping me too.

We discuss the idea and I concede that living alone is not the best thing for me or my recovery. 'There'll be no pressure,' she says. 'You won't have to talk. You just have to come and stay, and there will always be a bed for you and a plate of food.'

I'm grateful but reticent. 'Okay,' I say. 'It's a kind offer. And maybe . . .'

At the back of my mind are doubts. That niggling fear – persistent and intractable – that tells me I can't go anywhere in case I feel trapped.

But Pippa is gently persistent. 'I've got lasagne for supper tonight. Come over if you fancy a bite to eat,' she says casually.

Later I find myself looking at Ella and saying, 'Maybe we should go. We need a walk anyway.' So we wander over, all the dogs and me, and have such a lovely evening we end up staying the night.

I wake up next morning feeling that the healing process with my family has begun, but knowing, too, that my parents are still grappling to understand what has happened to me.

Meanwhile, CBT is retraining my mind, and my therapist – circumventing house rules, which do not allow dogs in the building – kindly welcomes Ella into my sessions. We smuggle her in via the basement stairs so the receptionist is unaware of the infringement.

My therapist knows how vital my dogs are to my mental well-being – what a pivotal role Ella is playing in my recovery – and many of the exercises I am set revolve round dogs. I love the CBT. It is constructive and effective, not least because dogs are at the heart of it.

I realise that working with Boomf has added to my anxiety. In fact it has fed my depression. I am on temporary leave from work, but I do not feel I can return. I talk to one of the directors; he supports my decision to step away permanently, and I'm overwhelmed with gratitude. So the company carries on trading without me.

At the same time, not working is also panic-inducing. I need to earn a living. Fortuitously, a friend tells me that a pet company he knows is looking for a consultant who is knowledgeable about animals. I'm offered an interview.

Immediately the old lack of self-esteem creeps in. 'I don't really know that much,' I say inwardly. 'I'm not sure I'm capable of doing it,' I tell Dr Pereira. He points out that actually this is exactly my area of expertise and what I'd love to do. So I steel myself to pursue it.

At my next CBT session, I go through the process of applying for the consultant's job. I think about what might happen; the questions I'll be asked. And armed with the confidence and knowledge I've gained, I set off for my interview. It is in Farringdon, a one-and-a-half-hour walk – six or so miles – from our flat.

I take Ella, of course; we walk briskly, and all the way there I talk her through what I'll say at the interview.

When we reach the building, north of the river and just outside the bounds of the City of London, it is bustling with activity. The receptionist leaves her desk to stroke Ella, and it breaks the ice. Already I'm less nervous.

The interview is, in fact, more of a chat. I talk the entire time about my dogs. To begin with I think this soliloquy is just a preamble, but then I realise I've continued to talk about them without pause, and suddenly the time is up and I'm asked: 'When can you start?'

I feel relief that I've been offered the job – which is actually my passion – just by being myself. I'm to have a contract for eight months and will work a few days a week. I can't tell you how happy I am.

This is the first interview I've had – other than one to pick strawberries – because I've always worked for myself. This boost to my self-esteem makes me feel buoyant. To add to my delight, I've been told I can bring my dogs to work, and I've spotted a little park next door where I can walk them during breaks and lunchtimes.

Ella and I walk back home, she sensing my sunny mood, and when she picks up a waft of cooking from a little market in Farringdon selling all kinds of food, we make a detour and I buy two celebratory Mexican wraps.

Mine is full of spiced mince, beans and rice. The chef laughs when I ask for a doggy-sized one for Ella with plain chicken filling.

Our happy mood continues as we munch away. I'm already excited about this new challenge, but there are doubts, too, as my anxiety runs deep. Having secured the job, I now really need to prove myself.

But the worries turn out to be groundless. It emerges that I not only enjoy my new role, but also, it seems, make some valuable contributions. I feel my confidence slowly coming back.

There is, however, no shortcut to recovery. I've been prescribed methylphenidate (Ritalin) for my ADD, which I'm told contains a stimulant. This seems counterintuitive. But I'm assured the drug will help me complete tasks instead of leaving a trail of unfinished projects. It does make a positive impact, although I notice its benefits incrementally. I find I'm whittling away my to-do list, which is getting shorter by the day, steadily working my way through jobs I would have previously found daunting or insurmountable. I still take Ritalin today if I feel I need it.

I'm eager for each day to start. I sleep through the night instead of waking after a few hours in a cold sweat of panic. I look forward to my new job rather than dreading the deep, burning anxiety of being alone with my thoughts.

Pippa and Catherine, meanwhile, knowing the mental chaos I've endured during the darkest year of my life, are encouraging me to go on a holiday. A villa on Mustique has unexpectedly become vacant, and they dispatch me there for a week of rest and recuperation.

Mustique is as inaccessible as any of the Caribbean islands. You reach it by boat or propeller plane from one of the larger islands – I fly from St Lucia – and its sandy beaches and little coves are hidden and peaceful, its luxury villas discreet. Princess Margaret had a house there, built on a plot of land, a wedding gift from her friend Colin Tennant, who bought the island as a wilderness in 1958 for £45,000. It is a perfect place for my restorative break.

I'm on my own, which suits me, but at mealtimes I joke to the staff: 'Can you stop laying my table for one? It looks so sad,' so they set two places and tease me: 'Has your date stood you up again?'

The holiday over, the chance arises to join the crew of a sailing yacht en route to Antigua. It is a measure of how far I've come that I'm confident that with my sailing expertise I'll be a useful member of the crew.

But the seas are heavy and the winds strong. A few hours after we leave our anchorage, I'm throwing up on the leeward side, regretting being free-spirited James and wishing I'd just flown home as planned.

Once I find my sea legs, though, I start to enjoy the spray and swell; even the thunderous waves are exhilarating. And when it's calm, I fish off the side of the boat.

We arrive in Antigua to Caribbean sunshine, and I book my flight home for the next day. My family, ever watchful, have found me a hotel where a family friend happens to be staying. They tell me to keep an eye open for him.

Meanwhile, as chance would have it, it's 'White Night' at the hotel, which means that all the women are dressed like brides and the men are decked out like Travolta in *Saturday Night Fever*.

What to do? I rifle through the crumpled clothes in my rucksack and find a pink linen shirt and some pale trousers. I don't look right, so I ask for a table in a dark corner, and I'm sitting there trying to look small and inconspicuous when I hear a confident voice cry out, 'Hi, James!'

It's the family friend.

I'm yearning for an early night, having barely slept on the boat, and had planned to go to bed after dinner. But instead I find myself in animated conversation with this genial stranger – it turns out he's John, a friend of my parents, who lives in the next-door village – for the very good reason that we both love dogs.

The talk turns to spaniels, and to Ella in particular. John asks me if I'd help train his spaniels. I say I'd be delighted.

The evening passes swiftly as we talk about our passion for dogs, and I even find myself sharing the details of my depression. John is the first person I have confided in outside of my therapists and the family, but he invites such confidences as he is kind, a good listener.

I wonder if he'll make his excuses and disappear when the talk turns to mental health. Actually, he tells me it's interesting, which emboldens me to talk more.

Then I feel vulnerable, having told this stranger so much, and wonder if he'll report back to my family. But before I can stress that our conversation is confidential, he reassures me: 'It's wonderful that you feel able to speak about your depression, but don't worry. I won't be saying anything.'

It's 2 a.m., and the barman has long since disappeared (leaving a bottle of rum on the table for us to share) when we finally say our goodnights with a bear hug. I do not know it yet, of course, but when the time comes for me to start my own dog food business, it is John who becomes my partner. From this serendipitous chance meeting, a long-lasting association is formed.

If only I could then have just gone back to my room to sleep. But there is a problem. I've forgotten my room number, all the staff have gone off duty and my plastic keycard holds no clue to where I'm staying.

The hotel is comprised of a series of apartments spread over a vast acreage, and I've been given a bicycle to get about. But in my rush to go to dinner, I failed to get my bearings. Every apartment looks identical, and I cycle round in the dark for an hour, trying not to look suspicious, before I finally find my room, identifying it by the trainers on the doorstep. I flop into bed shortly before dawn and sleep.

Back home in London, I'm starting to think that the ideal next business venture for me would be dog-related.

It has always been my mantra that the best thing you can do for your dogs is feed them the best possible diet.

I start to experiment with giving my dogs a raw diet. The little freezer at our flat is crammed with meat. I blend it with vegetables and the dogs love it. I'm enthused – and the dogs signal their approval by licking their bowls completely clean.

I also reflect again on the inestimable help Ella and my other dogs have given me, not only in my recovery from mental ill health, but also in calming, comforting and supporting me through so many events, from the everyday to the momentous.

I had read about emotional support animals in America and concluded that the idea – though well meant when it was conceived – had got out of hand. Apparently, someone once insisted on taking their emotional support peacock on board a plane.

In the UK we have a wonderful charity, Pets As Therapy (PAT), which recognises the capacity of animals to enrich our lives and enhance our health and well-being, and strives to give adults and children in hospitals, care homes, prisons and a multitude of other places access to friendly and well-mannered dogs and cats.

Wouldn't my beloved Ella be an ideal candidate to cheer up those without a pet? I offer our services; they are accepted, and I find myself on my way to Manchester Children's Hospital.

There, a nurse who has a therapy dog herself, shows me the ropes. I'm nervous about going onto the wards, but Ella is not. Nothing – neither the unfamiliar surroundings nor the curious smells – fazes her. We knock on doors.

'We have a dog. Would you like to see her?'

Invariably the answer is a resounding 'Yes!' Sometimes it's confident; at other times shyer and less assertive.

We see children who are too ill to get out of bed and the nurse sets up protective sheeting that allows Ella to jump up beside them. There is no breaking the ice. It is straight in with the questions.

'What's her name?' 'How old is she?' 'Does she do tricks?'

The delight and curiosity is overwhelming. Ella is wearing a little Pets As Therapy bandana round her neck. It endears her even more to the children, who are thrilled by it. She adores the attention and proffers her head to be stroked.

We go from bed to bed, and one child is particularly upset. She does not want to go for her X-ray. One of the nurses has an idea. 'What if Ella comes with you?'

I give a thumbs-up, and the child's sad face breaks into a smile. 'Really? Can she actually come with me?'

'Of course she can,' I say, and so we make a space on the bed where Ella can sit as the young patient is wheeled down the corridor.

When we get to the X-ray room, the nurse tells her: 'When you come out, Ella will be waiting for you,' and the little girl, reassured, goes off happily.

Twenty minutes later, she is back and smiling as she spots Ella, who rides with her to the ward, being fussed and stroked all the way.

These are simple moments, but the reward is disproportionate. To see a child's nerves calmed, their anxieties dispelled, their attention distracted and their face break into a wide smile all because of a friendly, sweet-natured dog is heart-warming. It is as therapeutic for me as it is for the patients.

We go into the intensive care wards and I take a deep breath. There are children hooked up to wires, drips and heart monitors, their anxious parents sitting at their bedsides sober-faced and preoccupied.

Then Ella patters in on her lead. We approach one bed and I see the child's heart rate rise with the excitement: 'A dog!'

'And she looks just like Grandma's Polly, doesn't she?' puts in her mum, her face now alert and smiling. 'But Polly wouldn't be allowed here because she's too naughty.'

A nurse bustles in, self-contained, propelled by the urgency of her task. Then she spots Ella, and suddenly she is kneeling down and cuddling her, not even acknowledging me.

'I needed that,' she says as she gets up, straightens her back and smiles, and I realise it is not just the patients but the staff too who take solace in animal visitors and a brief respite from the pressure of their jobs.

Coming back to London on the train, I feel my eyes blur with tears. I'm not a father, but I think about those children in hospital and I reflect on how lucky I am.

Ella looks at me, sensitive to my pensive mood. She has achieved a small everyday miracle. She has, even if only for a few brief minutes, dispelled parents' worries and lifted sick children's spirits just by being herself.

I think about the three-fold benefits of PAT. Ella, the children and I all felt the value of that hospital visit. I resolve to encourage more pet-owners to sign up with the charity. I think, too, that a new chapter in Ella's life has begun.

Without her, I could well be just an inscription on a tombstone. She saved me from my lowest ebb, and now she is spreading her love to others.

Chapter Nine
Ella Plays Cupid

———

If you'd told me in my darkest moments that within a year of contemplating ending my life I would have met my future wife, I'd have been annoyed; infuriated that anyone would suggest that fortunes could change so abruptly, that it could possibly be true.

My mind was starting to heal, my parents were breathing a tentative sigh of relief, but the last thing on my mind was finding a girlfriend.

One of the challenges – rarely discussed – about clinical depression and anxiety is that it dampens libido. You don't feel motivated about sex when your life is overhung by a black cloud.

The prescription antidepressants I was then taking – although I was initially resistant, I conceded that I needed them, but only as a temporary measure to see me through the bleak early days of my illness – also added to the problem. Not the most auspicious start when you're dating.

I'd started seeing someone in a half-hearted way early in 2018. We'd been out for dinner and I had to take my medication – which I tried to do subtly – with food. My date, seeing me furtively swallow my pills, asked me what I was taking and why.

I tested the water a bit. 'It's for my mental health.'

Her reaction floored me: 'Oh, I hope you're not going to be like my ex. He had all sorts of issues. He was one of those complicated guys.'

I was taken aback. 'Oh, no, no. It's just to help me keep on top of stuff,' I blundered.

I never saw her again. A relief really, as I don't think she'd have been remotely sympathetic about the libido problem. Besides, I'd already made up my mind that she wasn't right for me and was about to make my excuses.

So I decided it was far too early to start dating. What I needed to do was focus on myself and on getting well.

But then in the summer of 2018, everything changed.

I've had an early-evening meeting to discuss my potential dog food idea at the South Kensington Club. Everything has gone well. My mood is buoyant.

Ella is with me; we're both familiar with the surroundings – the club is quite near our flat, so we often come here together – and we sit out on the balcony on this balmy evening, enjoying the warmth.

It gets to nearly 6 p.m. I'm off to Stockholm the next day to visit friends who have one of my puppies, Pickle. (They were meant to have poor Mini, but chose another from a subsequent litter after she died.)

Knowing I have a busy weekend ahead, I toy with going home but decide to stay for a quick beer and pick up some food for dinner on the way home.

I wait for the waiter. Ten minutes pass, then fifteen. He doesn't come by. Then a young woman, slender, with a rippling river of golden blonde hair, rushes in and joins a female friend who has been waiting at a corner table.

I notice the latecomer particularly because Ella has wandered across the balcony and is sitting down, obstructing her path so she has to walk round her. The young woman greets her friend with a hug and they start chatting.

Another ten minutes or so pass and I am still waiting fruitlessly. Meanwhile the friends are looking at the drinks menu and scanning the room for the elusive waiter too.

And that's when I see that Ella has walked over to the slender blonde woman and has not left her side. The woman, in turn, has started to make a fuss of her.

I'm hoping she's not annoyed by my persistently friendly dog, so I jump up and go over to apologise. But by this time Ella is lying blissfully on her back having her tummy tickled.

'I'm really sorry. I hope Ella isn't bothering you,' I blurt.

The blonde woman looks up. She has beautiful eyes and a warm smile. She says in a mesmerising French accent: 'No, no, not at all! But we're still waiting for a drink. We'd like a Pinot Noir and a Sauvignon Blanc.'

I realise then that in my haste to retrieve Ella, I've walked across the balcony still clutching the drinks menu. The charming French woman thinks I'm the waiter.

I don't disabuse her of the idea. I just go inside to the bar and order drinks for her and her friend, and a beer for myself.

I'm caught off balance, captivated. I don't quite know what has happened to me. I walk back outside and sit sipping my beer; then, realising that time's getting on, I remind myself I have to get home and pack for my visit to Stockholm.

Back at the bar, I tell the waiter I'd like to pay for the drinks for the two women sitting outside. He looks at me as if I'm slightly mad. 'Well, I assumed so. After all, you ordered them,' he replies, genial but confused.

Then he asks: 'Who shall I say paid for them?'

'Give me a moment.'

I ask him for a piece of paper, grab a pen and, on impulse, compose a little note, searching for the right words as I go along.

'Hi, So I don't usually do this,' I begin, 'in fact this is the first time that I have and I realise it's slightly more difficult to figure out what to say than I thought. Anyhow, here goes.

'I have no idea if I'm barking up the wrong tree and forgive me if I am, but I was wondering if you might like to go for a drink sometime, or maybe in the future. Here is my number.

'It would be lovely to hear from you. Absolutely no pressure to reply but hope you have a lovely evening.'

And I sign it 'James and Ella', adding, for clarity, '(dog)'.

Rereading it, I cringe. For a moment my courage falters: should I send it or not? I look at Ella for reassurance and ask her, 'What have I got to lose?'

And then, before I can change my mind, I say to the waiter: 'When they ask for their bill, would you give them this note?' Suddenly panicking, I realise it could end up in the wrong woman's hands, so I emphasise: 'It's for the one on the left.'

I fold the note, hand it over. The waiter smiles. I smile back.

'I'm going to have to go now, otherwise I'll change my mind,' I say out loud, half to Ella, half to myself.

And then I walk down the street thinking, 'What on earth have I done?'

Back at home, I prepare some food, eat; calm down a bit. Then the qualms rush in again. Oh my God, James. What an idiot you are. She barely acknowledged you and now she's reading a random note from a total stranger she mistook for the waiter.

At 10.30 p.m., as I am busy packing my carry-on bag for the flight to Sweden, a message pings through on my phone. Unknown number. Oh. Okay. I open it: 'Hi, James, thanks so much for your message. Very sweet of you. I would love to go for a drink with you and Ella. I'm around at the weekend.'

She has signed it 'Alizée'.

My heart does a joyful little somersault.

Then I think, 'Oh no!' I hadn't actually planned for the wonderful eventuality that she'd accept immediately and suggest this coming weekend. I pace the room.

What do I do? I'm about to get on a plane to Stockholm. Then I'm off to New York for work for a week. And this gorgeous girl with a mesmerising French accent has accepted my invitation to go for a drink just when I'm leaving London.

The only time I'll have is a brief few hours on Sunday evening after getting back from Sweden and before leaving for the USA early Monday morning.

Sunday night. Normally I'd be in my pyjamas ready for bed by 8 p.m. But I can't pass up the opportunity to see Alizée again.

'Lovely to hear from you!' I reply breezily. 'Would Sunday evening work for you?' I hit 'send' before I can start finding reasons why it won't work for me.

I close my eyes. Put the phone down. Try to continue packing. I'm completely flustered. I don't get a response that evening, and I try to work out how to pronounce Alizée. Is it like Elise with an A? Or maybe Al-easy? I try out a few options.

I go to bed leaving my phone by my pillow, messages not silenced, just in case she replies.

My alarm wakes me. No new messages. Damn it.

I take Ella to stay at Pippa's. In the taxi to the airport, a thousand thoughts course through my mind. Have I been too forward? Have I messed up? Chosen the wrong day of the week? After all, who goes out on Sunday evening?

I'm just about to board the plane when a message pings through. 'Sunday is perfect. How about 6 p.m.? Let me know where you'd like to meet.'

Oh hallelujah!

By the time I land, I've prepared my response.

'How about meeting at this little hotel – Blakes – for Sunday evening drinks at 6.30 p.m.? Have a lovely weekend and look forward to then.'

I have a fantastic time with my friends in Sweden, swimming, boating, enjoying seeing Pickle settled happily in her home. My friends know about my depression and are delighted I'm so much better.

On Sunday I head back to the airport with a spring in my step. I'm going to see Alizée.

But as I bound into departures, I'm confronted by the message every traveller dreads: 'Flight delayed'. My mood plummets. An hour and a half's delay. I might not get back for my date.

I make a few mental calculations. I should scrape in just in time, if nothing else goes wrong.

I get through security, am waiting to board, willing everything to go smoothly.

Then another announcement: 'Flight delayed by two hours'.

What do I do? If I send Alizée an apologetic text, will it look as if I've bailed out before we've even started?

The queue to board shuffles sluggishly forward. I'm almost herding everyone on. 'Let's go, let's get on the plane,' I urge them inwardly.

At last we're sitting down and the captain is announcing smoothly that we'll be able to make up some time and won't be delayed for more than an hour and a quarter. Hurrah!

At Heathrow, I run through the concourse, lungs bursting, jump onto a Tube into London and tap out a message to Alizée: 'I'm so sorry. Can we make it 7 p.m.? Flight delayed.'

Back comes her reply: 'Thank goodness! I was going to suggest 7 p.m. too.'

I'm almost bursting with relief.

But then when I get off the Tube, I realise I haven't got time to pick Ella up from Pippa's. I'll have to go straight to Blakes. I jog the last 30 minutes to the hotel, wiping sweat off my forehead and tucking in my shirt as I try to amble nonchalantly through the front door. To my huge relief, Alizée has not yet arrived.

I request a discreet corner table, go to the bathroom, try to tame my tangled hair with my hands, splash my face with water.

I walk back to the table – willing my thudding heart to calm – and sit down, mustering an expression of equanimity.

Then in walks golden-haired Alizée, a burst of sunshine. Oh shit! I squirm inwardly. I haven't worked out how to pronounce her name.

'Hi, so lovely to meet you!' I say, giving her a little Gallic peck on each cheek. Then I plunge in, breaking the ice with 'I wanted to ask you how your name is pronounced.'

'Al-i-zay,' she explains. (The accent is as charming as I remembered.) 'Actually it's the French for "trade wind". My father loves sailing and windsurfing and he wanted to call me after that.'

Okay, I think. Sailing and windsurfing. We're off to a good start.

Then she asks: 'Where's Ella?'

She's remembered!

'The only reason I agreed to come was to see her again,' she smiles. 'The invitation was to have a drink with James and Ella.'

So I tell her that I didn't have time to go to my sister's to pick Ella up, and she smiles, appeased by the fact that there's a legitimate excuse.

And then we settle with our drinks and don't stop chatting. We barely pause. Something close to a miracle has happened.

Alizée goes to the bathroom and I think, 'This is too good to be true. Everything she says, her interests, her values; we are so aligned. Is there a catch? Is this just a dream?'

Hours later, the bar staff politely tell us they have to close. They don't want to kick us out, but they're going to have to stop serving us drinks.

To our surprise, the evening has passed in a blink and it's midnight. Alizée has work on Monday – she works in the City, in financial technology – and I'm off to catch my flight. It's time to say goodnight.

I don't want to look overly keen; equally I can't leave her without a promise that we'll meet again. I walk her to her place in Kensington, giving her a little goodbye kiss on both cheeks again. 'Let's be in touch and arrange another date,' I say, as casually as I can, and she smiles and agrees we should.

I'm walking home, buoyed by euphoria, when I realise I ought to check my phone – silenced during the evening – to see if there are any messages.

Twenty-eight missed calls. All from Pippa.

'When are you coming to collect Ella?'

Then, 'James, where are you? It's getting late and I want to go to bed. Are you coming to get Ella?'

And so the messages continue, escalating from concern to irritation.

Oh God. Forgetting Ella. It's unprecedented. Only Alizée could induce that kind of temporary amnesia.

Pippa and James live a ten-minute walk from me. I rush round, arriving breathless and apologetic on their doorstep. James answers the doorbell. Ella is at his side, looking mildly reproachful. James gives me a curious smile.

'So sorry,' I stammer, looking contrite and giving Ella a nuzzle. 'I'll get going so you can go to bed.' No questions are asked, but James's quizzical look suggests he suspects something.

Back at the flat, I throw clothes into a holdall, packing as quickly as I can because I've got to get up at 4 a.m. to drive Ella to Bucklebury, where my parents, already looking after my other dogs, will be caring for Ella too.

I barely sleep. All night I go over every nuance of my conversation with Alizée. Did I say anything silly? Was I too keen?

Ella seems perplexed. It's unusual for me to be leaving so soon after arriving home. I give her a big hug, tell her I'm really sorry and promise I'll be back in a week. 'And then I'll be all yours again and you'll get lots of attention,' I reassure her.

I tell her, too, that I'm sorry I didn't take her on the date with Alizée. After all, I promised, and Ella played such a pivotal role in introducing us. 'But next time,' I say.

I think she senses something different about me. Perhaps it is just the hint of a new scent – Alizée's – that gives her a clue, or the lightness of my mood. She knows, of course, that I am happy.

Next day, as a hopeful dawn breaks, I drop her at Bucklebury, knowing she'll be well cared for in my absence, and drive to the airport. Before I get on the plane, I compose a message to Alizée: 'Hope you made it to work okay. Great getting to know you. I'm back at the weekend. Let me know if you're about. Perhaps we could go for dinner?'

I press 'send' hoping I've struck a balance somewhere between casual and overeager.

That week, we exchange messages. All seems to be going well. Towards the end of my trip, I tell her about the Lake District.

'We should go.'

'Yes, that would be great.'

'How about next weekend?'

No reply for a while. Damn it. Have I been too insistent? Perhaps Alizée just thought it was a vague invitation: 'We should go one of these days.' I agonise over every syllable of our text conversation.

Then a response pings back.

'One more proper date before we go away for a weekend,' she says.

So once I'm back from New York, we meet for a drink at my local London pub, The Cross Keys, and this time Ella comes too. It's even better than the first date, except that I'm nervous, anxious that paparazzi don't spot us and scare Alizée off before I've even had a chance to explain why they could be lurking around.

But the pub staff are discreet, nobody sees us and Ella loves the attention Alizée is lavishing on her. We go back to my flat and I cook dinner – miraculously without mishap – and then I show Alizée some pictures of the Lakes.

I'm eager to make plans. I tell her about the walk Ella and I will take her on. Our favourite mountain walk. The one I've done hundreds of times before.

We pick a weekend when we're both free, and the date is set. I'm counting down the days.

On the Friday evening we've plumped for, in September 2018, I'm so keen not to be late that I arrive with the dogs to pick her up just as she's coming home from work. 'Let me have a shower. I'm pretty much packed,' she smiles, and I wait in the car.

Fifteen minutes later, she emerges with a bag, hair still damp, a pair of walking boots slung over her shoulder and a big grin lighting up her face.

'I hope you have a good playlist,' she says as we settle in for the journey, and we're off, driving through the night to the cottage where so many of my happy childhood memories were formed.

It's a pitch-black, starless night when we arrive; an autumnal nip in the air that chills. I set to and light the fire and lamps, open a bottle of wine, put some cheeses on a plate. It is snug and warm by the time we climb the stepladder to bed and settle into our sleeping bags.

I wake early to an overcast day, coax the fire into life, let out the dogs and cook a hearty breakfast. By the time we're ready to set off on our walk – cheese and tomato sandwiches packed, with some red wine decanted into an empty water bottle – the cloud has lifted. There is the promise of sunshine; the air is clear and the trees a blaze of russet and red glory.

We chat as we walk, and when we get to a kissing gate, familiar to me as all the landmarks on this favourite walk are, I pause and decide to try my luck.

'You have to kiss when you go through this gate.'

A deep stare from Alizée; a quizzical smile. No invitation.

'Okay then. Just a peck on the cheek if you prefer,' I say.

We're on either side of the gate and I get just that. And a laugh from Alizée, who clearly thinks I've invented this tradition.

The walk continues, and I realise with every step how perfectly attuned we are. I sense a familiar yet buried feeling; I think I am falling in love. There is something extra special about Alizée: about the way she gets on with my dogs and they clearly warm to her; about her love of long hikes in wild countryside on cold, bright autumn days; about how she settles so happily into the tiny cottage where we stay, embraces the primitiveness of it. I pinch myself and think I can hardly believe it. I already know – hope – that she will be part of my life for ever. And the thing that settles it for me is when she jumps into an icy rock pool straight after I do, laughing.

I do not know if the tingly rush of pleasure I feel when I hit the water is caused by my thudding heart or the shock of the chill, but yes, I think it must be love.

During the weekend, I tell Alizée about my mental health issues. I broach the subject during a walk when she is talking about the pressures of work and she mentions a suicide.

We talk about the numbers of young men in particular who take their own lives. Then I tell her I've had clinical depression and she asks if I've recovered.

'Actually, it's not something you ever overcome completely,' I say. 'We all have to look after our mental health, just as we do our bodies, by sleeping, exercising and eating properly.'

She encourages me to talk and is delighted by my honesty. She does not regard it as a complication, and I feel very comfortable talking to her. She is neither dismissive nor put off, but genuinely interested and keen to learn.

This is a comfort to me; another reason why I feel she is exactly the right person for me.

On the drive home, she falls asleep next to me and I glance across at her. 'Can I be in love yet?' I ask myself. 'Can it actually happen that quickly?'

I put on *Harry Potter*, quietly, so I do not wake her. I'm nearing the last chapter of this epic series of books I love so much, and the last sentence resonates: 'All was well.'

'All *is* well,' I think to myself. 'All is actually very well.' My dogs are breathing heavily as they snooze. Alizée is sleeping peacefully next to me. The serotonin high I feel is, I know, associated with falling properly in love.

Another reassuring thing about Alizée is that she knew nothing about my connection with the monarchy until I tentatively mentioned it. This was not out of disrespect for the institution, but because she has lived a nomadic life on several different continents and has not followed the day-to-day goings-on of our royal family.

Her father, a diplomat with the French embassy, has worked all around the world. During her childhood, Alizée lived in Germany, Chile, Indonesia and Belgium; she speaks five languages fluently.

So although she recalls Catherine and William's wedding, she does not remember a little brother reading a lesson in the service. And now she does know, she is not fazed, concerned or remotely overawed.

We spend a glorious golden autumn together. Alizée forms a special bond with Mabel, and sometimes when I look at the two of them crunching through the leaves together on a country walk – Alizée in a trench coat, her river of blonde hair echoing the colour of Mabel's fur – I think I have captured my own ray of sunshine.

My blackest time has passed. I am moving from darkness into light.

Four happy months pass together. We share meals out, walk and shop, go to a carol service. Nobody seems to notice us in our blissful bubble.

Ella – my faithful guardian – has already accepted Alizée, even before conversation turns to a permanent relationship. Ella used to sleep on my bed. Now she knows that Alizée shares it with me and she adjusts to sleeping on her own bed on the floor right next to us.

She does not object to this new arrangement. In fact she knows she is making way for someone who makes me very happy indeed.

Chapter Ten

The Healing Power of Dogs

Alizée is living with me now, sharing our family flat, and I still can't believe this waking dream is real, that she actually wants to be with me.

We fit so well together. Our thoughts and hopes are in perfect synch. And during the autumn – when the whole world seems vibrant with colour and happiness seeps through my veins – we decide it is time we introduced each other to our families.

Alizée's family, being in France, don't come over en masse, but there's a succession of visits: her brother, an uncle and aunt, grandparents and, of course, her parents. If I didn't know better, I'd think they had all conspired to inspect *l'homme anglais* and report back to each other!

Because Alizée works from her office and I often do my consultancy work from home, I offer to greet her grandparents, our first visitors, at the airport and drive them into London.

So that's why I'm here now, at Heathrow, meeting the flight from Lyon with a photo of *grandmère et grandpère* clutched in my hand, frantically scanning the elderly folk tottering through arrivals to see if any of them match the image in front of me.

Finally I spot them, but my challenge is only just beginning. I dust off a few greetings from my (very limited) repertoire of schoolboy French. (Alizée's grandparents are in their eighties and do not speak English.)

'*Bonjour!*' I call, adding (I think) that I hope they've had a pleasant journey. But some Spanish words get inadvertently intermingled in my sentence. Grandmother, who hasn't a clue what I'm saying, perks up a bit when she recognises the Spanish, imagining I must speak the language, and tries out a sentence in Spanish on me.

But I have even less idea about Spanish than French, and by the time we've reached the car, we're convulsed with helpless giggles. Fortunately the laughter continues for the whole journey home.

Neither of us has the remotest idea what the other is saying, but our shared universal vocabulary of laughter and gesticulations sets the mood of hilarity, and by the time we reach The Cross Keys – where by happy coincidence Alizée is just coming through the door – we're all in a jolly mood.

It is the prelude to a happy evening. I'm relieved we get on so well, and I'm more confident when I go to meet Alizée's uncle, whose English, fortunately, is fluent. We also get along brilliantly. Next time it is her parents – her father, Jean Gabriel, now retired from the diplomatic service, and her mother, Laurence – who fly over. They navigate their own way into London and I walk down the road to meet them from the Tube.

Alizée is speaking to her mother on the phone when I come into view. 'James is coming to find you,' she says.

'How will I recognise him?' asks her mum.

'Easy. He'll be walking along with four dogs.'

And then I hear a laugh. It's Laurence. She has just spotted the person who is unmistakably me and is waving. Not many people walk through London with so many dogs.

Having by now met most of the family – and found them all delightful – when conversation turns to Christmas and Alizée asks if I'd like to join them skiing in the French Alps, I'm bursting with excitement. Alizée, mountains, skiing: a matchless combination. 'That would be wonderful!' I say.

I can't wait to learn more about her and visit her grandparents' chalet, which is invested with so many of her happy childhood memories.

I speak to Mum about the prospect of going away for Christmas. She looks at me and for a moment I think she'll resist. Then her face breaks into a smile. She is delighted that after so many turbulent years I am at last finding happiness. I will go with her blessing.

Meanwhile Alizée has yet to meet my family. Her first encounter with them happens quite by accident.

We have been to a wedding not far from Bucklebury. It's a warm September weekend; we haven't brought an overnight bag, but we think we'd like to wake up to Sunday in the countryside, so rather than take a taxi back to London after the reception, we decide on impulse to stay overnight at Mum and Dad's. It's midway between the wedding venue and home.

Arriving late and unannounced, we let ourselves in and tiptoe around in the dark, not wanting to wake anyone, then catch a few hours' sleep before I'm woken at 7.30 a.m. by giggling at the bedroom door. It's George and Charlotte, my nephew and niece. I didn't realise that all three children are staying for the weekend with my sister and William.

Alizée is still sound asleep, so I gently shush the children and we go downstairs, where Catherine and William are drinking their early-morning tea. I'm about to take a cup up to Alizée when she appears at the kitchen door. She has just got out of bed, her hair still tousled, and she is wearing one of my shirts.

In situations like this, Alizée is wonderfully French. She does not panic or rush upstairs to get dressed. Instead she just greets everyone warmly as if it's not remotely unusual to be meeting her boyfriend's sister and brother-in-law for the first time wearing only an oversized man's shirt.

'Hello,' she says, proffering her hand, and with no awkwardness at all we're soon all chatting amiably and the children are asking all kinds of cheeky questions at a hundred miles per hour.

How come we weren't there when they went to bed? Why didn't they know we were coming? And who *is* this lady? Is she your girlfriend? (Cue giggles from both of them.)

So I tell Charlotte and George, yes, she is my girlfriend and introduce her to them, then we are all talking and laughing effortlessly as if she has been part of the family for years.

Later that afternoon, Mum and Dad, who've been away for the weekend, come home. The next day we go for a walk together, all of us, and the autumn mist feels not melancholy, but like a haze of happiness that wraps itself around us, enveloping us all.

It is wonderful to hear Dad and Alizée chatting together in French. Dad lived in Geneva for a year while studying for a degree in metallurgy (the scientific study of the structure and uses of metals). He worked as a bike courier to earn some extra money and became fluent in French while he was there. He always jumps at the chance to brush up on a language he loves.

We are a family of Francophiles: my paternal grandmother also learned French, during the war, when she worked at Bletchley Park, the principle centre for Allied codebreaking.

She met my grandfather during the war too, and there is a link to the royal family here as well, because Grandpa, who was a pilot, flew Prince Philip during a trip to Canada.

Now here is a new connection to a country we all love, in the form of Alizée. She and Dad talk about the Lake District, and Alizée is telling him how much she loved her visit there. Dad is smiling. Everything feels just right.

I knew my family would make Alizée welcome. What I feared was that they might overwhelm her. But she is not remotely overawed by our royal connection. Catherine and William are just my sister and brother-in-law as far as she is concerned, and she is delighted to spend a day with them.

So when we all hug goodbye, I get a special squeeze from Catherine, who whispers in my ear, 'She's just great,' and Mum's warm smile tells me she agrees. All my stars have aligned: Alizée is perfect for me and my family adore her too.

Alizée and I exist in our own blissful little world, untroubled by press intrusion – until, that is, we go to the annual Henry van

Straubenzee memorial carol service. Henry, whose brother Tom is Charlotte's godfather, died tragically young in a car crash, and the service is not just to remember him but to raise money for the school projects in rural Uganda he supported.

Belting out a carol signals the start of Christmas for me; the service is for a good cause, and although Alizée has been resisting any public outing and we know there might be photographers there, we decide to go along.

'We're going for the right reasons,' we both agree. Neither of us courts publicity or self-promotion; both of us abhor celebrity culture. But this special annual event seems the right place to be spotted together, as we know we will be eventually.

When we arrive, there is the expected posse of photographers, and Alizée, caught in their flash lights, is momentarily overwhelmed. I feel nervous; scared that the sudden jolt of publicity will put her off being with me.

The next day, one of the national newspapers publishes a photo of us together with a story. But they get Alizée's identity wrong, confusing her with someone I haven't even met. Alizée is unperturbed. She just laughs.

Knowing that there will be a bit of interest in finding out exactly who she is, we go undercover for a few days, keep ourselves to ourselves. There is plenty of speculation, but enquiries go unanswered.

I actually felt reassured when Alizée told me at the start of our relationship that my connection with the royal family made her less likely to go on a date with me, rather than more, but now I am concerned that the kerfuffle that accompanies my close affiliation with the heir to the throne might put her off me entirely.

She tells me, though, that it makes no difference at all. She has had time to get to know me now and she wants to be with me. She loves me for myself, not for any other reason. That fact alone makes me feel I am walking on air.

When I look back now, I am so glad I did not derail something so perfect by telling Alizée about Catherine's connections too soon. I'm pleased too that the first note I sent to her came from Ella and me; that she responded to us both without being encumbered by any preconceptions about me.

Then, by being discreet, we were able to get to know each other better. We did not go out to restaurants. We ate at home (giving us the chance to try lots of different recipes). We avoided conspicuous places, evaded gossip, and those early months were heaven.

Christmas in the Alps with her family is wonderful, too. We do not take the dogs – they stay with my parents' house-sitter at Bucklebury – but we have such fun and laugh so much; and I'm delighted when Alizée comes with my family to St Barts for New Year.

There is a single sour note. We are covertly photographed there kissing on a pontoon, a story runs in the British papers – by now the press has worked out who Alizée is – and she feels this invasion on her privacy keenly. It is a gratuitous intrusion during a private family holiday.

But now that our story is out, I reassure her, interest in her will recede. And of course it does.

There are times, however, when for the greater good it is important we tell our stories, and by January 2019, my mental health feels robust enough for me to speak publicly about it.

I steel myself to talk about the darkest year of my life, when I did not see the point of living any more. And I do so because I want to help dispel the stigma that surrounds depression and give hope to others who face the same bleak desperation that pushed me to the brink.

Suicide is the single biggest killer in Britain of young males under 45. It is a chilling fact that in the UK, 84 men in this age bracket take their lives every week. And I understand the blank despair that so often leads them to it.

The male suicide rate is disproportionately high: 15.8 per 100,000 compared with a female rate of 5.5 per 100,000.

These are terrifying statistics, but by speaking about them we help to lift the cloak of shame that for so long has enveloped mental health problems.

When it comes to it, I'm nervous about going public. How will the media interpret my story? How will readers respond? I am worried that people will think I'm an entitled former public schoolboy who shouldn't be complaining about his privileged life. How have I the right, blessed with so much good fortune, to admit to suffering terrible depression?

But the fact is, mental health problems affect the disadvantaged and the favoured indiscriminately.

Knowing I am about to take the plunge, I decide to set my Instagram account – which I've always kept private – to public. 'If I'm sharing my story, I want as many people as possible to know about it,' I tell Alizée.

I talk very openly to Frances Hardy from the *Daily Mail* – who has written this book with me – about the collapse of my mental health and my descent into despair. It feels at once liberating and frightening to have exposed my darkest thoughts.

The night before the publication of my article, I am sleepless with nerves. Alizée knows all about the piece, which is written in the first person, and has supported my decision to give this deeply personal account. But how will my parents, born in a different era, when it was considered both shaming and weak to admit to a mental breakdown, respond to it?

Alizée is due to go to Paris to visit a friend on the Saturday the article is being published. I'm apprehensive about being alone when it comes out, worried about the reaction it will provoke, so at the last minute I ask if I can go with her.

'Yes, of course!' she cries.

I book my seat on the 6 a.m. Eurostar, and by 8 a.m. we are pulling in to Gare du Nord in Paris.

I'm walking, coffee cup in hand, down the street when I feel my phone buzzing in my pocket. I'm reluctant to look at it. I ignore the constant alerts and pings.

At 11 a.m., Alizée is chatting to her friend and I cannot put off looking at my phone any longer. I scroll through my messages. There are literally hundreds of them – emails, texts and missed calls – and even more responses on social media.

Nervously I read the first of them. 'Thank you for sharing your story,' it reads. 'You have really helped my brother who felt suicidal.' There are many more saying, 'You have summed up exactly how I feel.' They continue in this vein: supportive, kind, empathetic, sometimes grateful.

The response is extraordinary, the outpouring of love humbling. There is not one critical comment, and I feel overwhelmed with relief and gratitude to the many people who have bothered to tell me I've helped them.

Then I ring Mum. I'm worried about her response. How will she cope with the lacerating honesty of the article? But before I can speak, she says, 'I'm so proud of you.' She tells me about the reassuring calls she has had from friends who've told her that they or family members have been through similar ordeals, sometimes silently.

I look across at Alizée, who knows how nervous I've been, and beam at her. Then I rush over and give her a big hug. 'Are you okay?' she asks, and when I tell her I'm great, she sighs with relief. 'Well done,' she says.

It is as if a burden has been lifted, and we breeze through the rest of the weekend with light hearts.

Back in London, the warm responses continue. As I walk in the park and supermarket, strangers stop me and thank me for sharing my story. Supportive letters arrive from people all around the world.

I am pleased I was so vocal about what I had been through. I realise now that talking was actually instrumental in making me better. Now I am glad to be helping others.

The best part of my life is happening now because I acknowledged my depression. If I had not talked, I would have taken a different path. I do not believe I would even be alive today.

And then there is Ella. I think about the vital role she has played. She has never left my side. I have talked to her, shared with her my deepest secrets, and she has loved me unconditionally.

Dr Pereira advised me: 'If you find things hard to talk about, try telling Ella.' So I did. And when you say something out loud – to a beloved dog who does not judge you – it feels, strangely and comfortingly, very different from saying it in your head.

Ella never reacted adversely; she did not make me feel stupid or small. Actually, it was a relief to talk to her, because my thoughts stopped clogging up my head and I started to address them.

So Ella heard everything. More, even, than Dr Pereira.

I realise, too, that the simple act of caring for her – walking her, feeding her – was crucial to my recovery. She needed me. I needed her. This reciprocity saved my life.

There is more I must thank Ella for. My work as a consultant in the pet industry has shown me that many of the brands selling dog foods are headed by people who have no interest in dogs at all. Some of them actually detest dogs.

My own dogs' well-being is central to my life. I would often mix up my own recipes, using food they love, and freeze them. I swiftly came to the conclusion that the best way to care for your dog is to feed them the highest quality diet.

Dressing dogs in little cashmere overcoats, buying them expensive leather leads – all of this is unnecessary. Your dog couldn't care less about these fripperies. But the thing that really makes a difference to their health and well-being is what they eat.

When I started to feed my dogs food I'd prepared especially for them, I noticed the new spring in their step, the glossy nap to their coats, the shine in their eyes. All the family started asking: 'Can we have some of your food for our dogs, too?'

So that is how my dog food company, now called James & Ella, began early in January 2019.

Encouraged by Alizée, Ella and I are also doing our best to help others with mental health problems. We visit the Mosaic Clubhouse in Brixton, a charity that supports adults with enduring mental health conditions, helping them regain the confidence and skills to lead productive, happy lives.

Again, I think back to myself a year earlier – to my self-imposed isolation; that abject fear that prevented me from leaving the flat – and empathise with all those for whom it is a huge ordeal to take that initial tentative step out of their homes.

On our first visit, the noticeboard at the Clubhouse welcomes not me but 'our special visitors Ella and Doug'. (Doug, it turns out, is a friendly pug.)

I've been taught how to present Ella. I must not put anyone under pressure to talk. If they want to, that's okay. If they don't, that's fine too.

I sit in a common room with Ella. A young man appears in the doorway. I smile. He looks away. Others come and go, fuss over Ella, who responds with delight.

I look over towards the door. The same young man is still standing there, shy, reticent. Eventually he comes into the room, barely noticed, as I chat to someone else about the dog they had as a child.

While I'm talking, I do not realise that Ella has slipped quietly away from my side, and when I look round to find her, she is sitting with her head on the sofa, next to the quiet young man, who is entranced by her.

Tentatively he reaches out a hand to touch her head, and a smile spreads slowly across his face.

Five minutes on, he and Ella are lying on the floor and he is stroking her tummy. Ten minutes later, he is chatting to me. We are due to leave, but I stay for another hour, learning about the young man's life.

By the time we say goodbye, we have become friends. Ella has had a wonderful time; I feel the glow of satisfaction that comes from helping someone whose condition I understand so well.

On the way home, I reflect that therapy dogs should be on prescription. The NHS would save millions. Dogs help heal traumatised minds. They bring comfort to the lonely. They encourage tongue-tied children – like the little boy I once was – because they offer no judgement. They just listen.

There is even a scheme, Read2Dogs, and it is such a wonderful way of engaging children and helping them to overcome their fear of reading out loud, I become fascinated. I offer Ella's services. She passes with flying colours and enjoys listening as children make their first faltering steps towards confident reading.

Ella and I go back to Brixton for more visits. We see our friend again. He writes to me and I keep in contact, sending notes back from Ella and me. He tells me of his ambition to have a dog of his own one day, and I reply that when the day comes, I will be there. I will help him.

I am always keen to spread the word about the joy dogs bring, and I'm happy to say that I also make a convert of one of the world's greatest tennis players.

Alizée and I have started to go to more public events together. Wimbledon is a favourite, as we both love tennis, and over the years

I've got to know Roger Federer and his wife, Mirka. Roger is, of course, a player of towering talent and charisma, but he is also a genuinely lovely guy.

They're a gorgeous family with four children – twin girls and twin boys – and when they come over for Wimbledon, they rent a house nearby, decamping there for the duration of the tournament with the children.

The girls are about nine, the boys five years younger, and Mirka is keen for them to feel at home during their extended stay in London, so we all go for walks together with my dogs.

The children are enchanted by the dogs and ask if one of them can go and stay for a little holiday with them. They're delighted when I say yes – if their mum and dad agree.

I don't really know how Mirka will respond – perhaps I shouldn't have made such a rash promise without speaking to her first, but within a few days she messages me: 'Are you serious about a dog coming to stay with us?'

I tell her I am. She says the kids will be bursting with excitement, that they've always longed for a dog and this will be a first step to see how they all get on.

I think hard about which of the pack will make the best house guest – knowing, of course, that I never let Ella out of my sight, so she is excluded – and conclude that Zulu will be ideal. He's a big softy and loves cuddles, but he also has a streak of mischief the children will enjoy, wagging his tail so fast it spins round and always claiming the best seat on the sofa.

So it is settled. Zulu will go to stay with the Federers for a week or so. I pack a little bag for him, gather up his bed and food, and we're off. Like a child going on his first sleepover with a friend, he's apprehensive to begin with, but once he sees the kids again, he's off like a rocket and doesn't look back.

I've written down his routine – feeding times, when he goes for walks – and I give it to Mirka, knowing he is in safe hands.

During his week away, I get regular updates on what he's been up to, with photos of his walks on Wimbledon Common. While Roger is playing tennis the children are forging a bond with Zulu and I'm certain that they're pleading with their mum for a dog of their own.

It isn't practicable while Roger is travelling, but a few months before he retires in 2022, he announces that they have welcomed Willow into their family, a beloved dog of their own, and I'm so pleased they've joined a worldwide community of dog lovers.

There are plenty of occasions, too, when I'm asked to help people with advice on their dogs' behavioural problems, and I'm gratified to do so whenever I can.

Alizée and I are at a drinks party in London and she is deep in conversation with Jimmy Carr, but when I ask, 'Do you know who he is?' she hasn't a clue.

'He's a comedian,' I tell her.

'Well he isn't that funny,' she replies.

I explain that his style is to deliver devastating one-liners in the most deadpan way (I don't think being French helps Alizée's understanding of his humour) and I go over to have a chat with Jimmy, who is affable company.

Before long – inevitably – we start talking about dogs. Jimmy has seen us out and about with our pack, and it emerges that he'd like some help with his two, who are proving quite a handful.

It's a genuine pleasure to me to share my knowledge and offer a few useful tips, which I also do on social media, as I get more questions about dog behaviour than anything else.

Alizée and I, meanwhile, are discovering so many things we share in common. We both love walking, so we set off together at a brisk pace to walk to work whenever we can.

The dogs can't wait to reach Battersea Park, where they'll have a run around before they are back on leads on the pavement, crossing the Albert Bridge as we make our way to the City.

It's a wonderful way to start the day – six bracing miles of exercise, rugged up against the chill of winter, then enjoying the early glimpses of pale spring sunshine – before a sedentary spell in the office.

But sometimes we're short of time, so Alizée suggests cycling and carrying the dogs in a little cart on the front of the bike. Cargo bikes. Some of her friends are taking their children to school in them. She shows me photos. It seems like a good idea to give it a go.

We take delivery of one and off I go with Ella for a spin to try it out. She loves it. She jumps in and we set off, her ears starting to lift as the speed picks up. It is a moment of pure ecstasy for both of us.

It's such fun that I ask myself: why haven't we thought of this before? All the dogs bundle in, their heads peeking over the top, and instead of trudging in a tangle of leads to the park, we're there in three minutes, Alizée pedalling beside me. We have bought ourselves some extra time for the dogs to have a scamper round on the grass.

Alizée uses a London hire bike to start with, but I think it's time she had her own. Mum has given me an old Peugeot cycle she had for a wedding present. It hasn't been used for about ten years so needs some substantial repairs and renovations, which I'm happy to carry out.

Having cleaned and serviced it, I present it to Alizée, She is thrilled. Her first car was a Peugeot, so it seems fitting that she is now cycling round on a Peugeot bike. I can hear her coming down the road on it – it has a distinctive clank and rattle – but this, she declares, gives it character. She is much happier with her restored vintage bicycle with its long family history than she would have been with a brand-new one.

The bicycles become our primary means of transport. This is how we commute to work, go shopping, go out to dinner with friends. Sometimes Alizée will decide not to cycle but will jump into the cart with the dogs, hair streaming as we weave through the traffic.

I know we look distinctive, Alizée and I, with our little menagerie of dogs in their carrier, but in the vast bustle of London, no one seems to notice our eccentricity.

By April we start to think about getting our own place together. The flat is wonderful but not ideal for a couple with four dogs, as it has no garden. We both like Battersea and we scour the estate agents for a place to rent.

One looks perfect, but they won't take dogs, so that's out. Eventually we find another that ticks all the boxes, though it doesn't specify whether it's pet-friendly. I ask the agent: 'How does the landlord feel about dogs?'

'I'll have to speak to him.'

Then, half an hour later, a phone call: 'Someone in the office is wondering how many dogs?' (This someone, it emerges, follows me on social media and knows I have four, sometimes five dogs – the fifth being Zulu, who still spends some of the time with Dad at Bucklebury.)

I admit I was not going to confess to this at once, just gently and by degrees: if he doesn't mind dogs in principle, how does more than one sound? Perhaps even several very well-behaved dogs?

As it is, I have to own up straight away to having four. And after some lengthy negotiations – and a promise that I'll put down a bigger than usual deposit – the house is ours. I've been living in the flat for 11 years; now, just 8 months after meeting Alizée, we are confident enough in our relationship to move in together.

When I contemplate that year, I cannot believe the change in my life. It is a rebirth. I've met someone I'm madly in love with, moved into a new house with her and started a new company doing something I'm really passionate about.

I want to give back to my dogs, who have given so much to me, and as I've always felt that diet is key to their well-being, this is how Ella & Co. (as it was called back then) started. My promise to dog-owners is to give them the confidence that they are providing their pets with the best nutrition and not being hoodwinked by clever branding.

When it comes to mental health recovery, there are no hard and fast rules about the pace of recovery. There are no guarantees that treatment will work. Everyone responds differently. But I know that everything I've been through has been worth it to reach this place of contentment.

I understand so much more about my mental health now. I am alert to signs that it may be compromised, and if it is, I try to declutter my mind. I don't burn the candle at both ends. I focus on the things that are really important to me. I make sure I am living in the here and now – very much as a dog does.

Dogs do not chase illusory goals or worry about what will happen tomorrow. They exist in the moment.

I have started to learn from my dogs. Now I am also better at stopping for a second and thinking: 'Wow, I've come a long way.' Just recognising that is a huge thing.

I think back to the day on the rooftop when Ella stopped me from taking my life. Can that transformation in me really have taken place in 12 months?

Chapter Eleven

A Father's Blessing . . . and a Proposal

———

Pippa and her husband James know how much I love the wildness and grandeur of Glen Affric. It has earned a special place in my heart, particularly since it played a formative role in my recovery.

So they suggest a part-time job for me, hosting weekend guests to the estate, which I can do in tandem with my dog food business – and I'm delighted to oblige, although I know how much I'll miss Alizée and hope I'll be able to persuade her to come up for visits as often as possible.

But much as I love this piece of beautiful countryside with its ancient pinewoods and loch flanked by towering mountains, December is a brutal month to introduce guests to its glories. And by now it is deep midwinter.

Our guests are prosperous people from all over the world – as well as Brits, there are Americans, South Africans, Europeans and Asians – and they all have something in common. They are looking for an extra dimension from their holiday. There is only so much a luxury hotel can offer, but at Glen Affric, alongside the comforts and intimacy of home, there is also the promise of adventures.

It is hard to entice them from the log fire in the lodge for a walk; harder still to convince them to take an icy dip in the loch. But I am enthusiastic. I want them to unwrap this new experience, to know how tingling with life they will feel if they brave their fears and go for a swim in water that is so cold it will make them gasp. Afterwards, the reward of sitting by the fire will be well earned; the sense of well-being even greater.

So there are those who trek with me and my dogs through forests and glens, and a few brave souls who experience the thrill of a winter swim.

During their stay, the silence and closeness of nature is healing. If you sit quietly enough, the wildlife forgets you are there. You might glimpse a shy pine marten sitting on a crag or a rare red squirrel trapeze-swinging through branches.

I've watched the aerial acrobatics of a golden eagle circling and swooping in a cobalt sky. At dusk, chevrons of geese fly overhead squawking. Bats swoop and dart, and a pair of night owls converse with a twit and answering twoooo.

We might glimpse an otter perched on rocks by the loch, where dragonflies flit in the summer. The mountains and forests are colonised by herds of red deer, and alongside the Scots pine, birch, rowan and alders grow, hosts to scarce species of lichen.

The pace of life slows here. There is no traffic to drown out the songbirds, and on a clear night, without pollution from street lights, you can lie on your back and count the stars.

I am here for three weekends in a row with the dogs but without Alizée, and I'm desperate to see her. I send her messages via photos of the dogs. One from Ella wishes her good luck in an interview. Another from Mabel invites her: 'Come and climb a mountain with us.'

Pippa and James are due to travel up the following weekend and Alizée joins them at Inverness, so they make the last leg of the journey together.

I'm excited to see her – it is a joy to be here, but with her by my side it will approach perfection – and I wait for her with heart-thudding excitement. I cannot wait to see her face.

She arrives, steps out of the car – and all the dogs rush forward to greet her. She fusses and strokes them, buries her head in their fur and nuzzles their ears, and suddenly I am aware that they are no longer my dogs, but ours, and Alizée has genuinely missed them.

Then she looks up, as if just remembering I'm there, beams and rushes over to hug me.

Pippa and James are mightily impressed by my petite French girlfriend. They marvel at the way she joins me for an early-morning dip with the dogs and smile as we all shake ourselves in a shiver of glistening droplets by the water's edge. When we emerge laughing, our teeth are chattering with cold.

They recognise that our passions are genuinely shared; they know we fit together like well-oiled gears. And now that I have taken ownership of my depression – I've talked about it, written about it – I have a new sense of confidence. I feel happier than I have ever been.

Much has happened since Alizée and I met, but we haven't yet had a proper holiday, just the two of us, and I suggest a sailing trip in March. There is a lot at stake. I haven't skippered a boat for a couple of years and now Alizée is urging me to do it.

It is also several months before the charter season starts in earnest – the waters of the Mediterranean are cold until June – but it is cheaper to go earlier, and as we are now saving to buy a house together, it seems sensible not to splash out needlessly.

So although there are fewer boats available, I find a 40-foot yacht, send off my credentials and references, pay the deposit and we're booked to go.

I dig out my yacht master notes to recap. I'm slightly nervous. Mum adds to my trepidation. 'Should you really be doing this, just the two of you?' she asks. She tells Dad. He calls me and runs through all his sailing tips on the phone.

Their anxiety infects me. I start to worry. Is this the most sensible thing to do, two of us renting someone else's boat for a week? I ask myself silently if I'm up to it.

But Alizée is excited and I try my best to dispel my fears and be excited too.

The boat is moored off Majorca and we fly there intending to sail round the island. Alizée draws up a shopping list of supplies and, oblivious to my fears, heads off to get them while I go off to the boat to be debriefed.

It is 5 p.m. before we're both on board, and we decide to spend a cosy first night in the harbour rather than leaving our anchorage in the dark.

It only occurs to me then that I have no idea what Alizée's sailing capabilities are. But you learn a lot from how someone moves around a boat, and she is deft and agile as a cat; I feel confident in her.

We share a bottle of wine with our meal, and next day, as the sun comes up, we drink our morning cups of tea then slip the lines from the jetty and motor out of the harbour. Within 20 minutes the sails are up, the engine off and we have set our course. Both of us have huge grins on our faces.

I feel glad that Alizée urged me to do this, that I overruled my fears. Five hours later, when we successfully anchor in a beautiful cove flanked by cliffs, on turquoise waters, putting a stern line to the shore to hold us in position, I am patting myself quietly on the back.

Putting an anchor down, as every sailor knows, is one of the most common causes of dispute. It is always someone else's fault if it goes wrong. But today we look like seasoned pros and everything goes exactly to plan.

Alizée puts together a delicious lunch, of sardines, cured meats, cheeses and olives with some grated vegetables. We eat it sipping a small glass of wine, after which we let down the ladder, go for a brisk swim then dry off in the sun.

Twice during our trip we anchor and go ashore, finding a quiet little bar for a beer, ambling around, picking up supplies.

Every time I tell myself I couldn't love her more, Alizée gives me another reason to do so. Without her encouragement I would never have chartered this boat. And now we are having more fun than we ever hoped.

For three more blissful days we sail on, but, realising that our planned schedule to circumnavigate the entire island is too ambitious, we decide to sail gently back, following the route we have already taken.

We arrive in the beautiful cove where we spent our second night, but this time two other boats are anchored there and it feels overcrowded. So we set anchor, but in deeper water, a little farther out of the bay.

That evening the swell picks up with a rising wind that lifts the boat. Just before sunset, the two other boats leave. I feel a pang of alarm.

I tune in to the weather forecast – in Spanish – picking up just a few words. As the night closes in and darkness descends, the temperature drops. We put on jumpers. By 10.30 p.m., we're thinking about bed. I let out more anchor chain, check the stern line. All is well.

We go to bed, but I set the alarm for midnight. I wake with the alarm, groggy with sleep, stumble onto the deck in buffeting winds and shine my torch on the anchor chain. It has given way. We cannot stay. It is too dangerous.

I tamp down my fears, try to stay calm. I wake Alizée and tell her we need to find a safer anchorage, as the wind is changing course and getting stronger. We must take shelter further into the cove, where we are less exposed.

We both set to and reposition the boat so we are in almost exactly the same place as we were on our outward journey. Observing the essential rituals, putting down the anchor, checking the chain, setting the stern line; these routines induce calm rather than panic.

We support each other, work as a team. The waves are swelling, the boat bucks and twists like a restive horse and I feel acutely my responsibility to protect Alizée, but she is composed, capable. The edge of danger does not make us touchy or abrasive. There is not a single sharp word or recrimination. We are bound by a shared sense of purpose: to secure the boat in rising seas, to stay safe.

There is something exhilarating about surmounting adversity as a team. It makes our partnership stronger. It is a formative moment in our relationship.

We do not sleep again until the early hours, and then only doze restlessly. In the morning we are up drinking tea, priming the boat for our five-hour voyage. When the sails are up, we fly back to harbour in a sharp wind. Our faces are smarting in the gale, but they are lit by huge grins.

Our sailing holiday has been a success, the ties that bind us strengthened by it.

We return to our house in Battersea buoyed up by happiness. This house, with *our* dogs, and *our* things; the friends who are *ours* rather than Alizée's or mine – all of this cements the feeling that we are now firmly a couple.

It is 2019, we've been together just a few months short of a year and I'm thinking of asking Jean Gabriel for his daughter's hand in marriage.

By chance, Alizée is talking about her parents coming over, and I encourage her to invite them. The weekend they are intending to visit, I am hosting in Scotland, and we arrange for them to come straight to Glen Affric. It feels like the perfect opportunity to speak to Jean Gabriel.

The weekend passes in a blur of happiness, of walks with the dogs, convivial meals and chats. But I just cannot get Jean Gabriel alone. I'm feeling twitchy with nerves, and whenever I think the right moment has arisen and the words are forming in my head, someone intrudes and I abandon the task.

Sunday evening and the end of their visit approaches. I have to devise a way to get Jean Gabriel away from everyone else. I cast around in my head for excuses.

'I need a hand to take down the sails on one of the boats on the loch. Would you help me?' I improvise wildly, knowing I don't need help and that it doesn't actually have to be done.

But Jean Gabriel is happy to oblige, and off we go – with Ella trotting at my heels in anticipation and encouragement – to reposition the boat and put it onto its mooring.

The boat is a Cornish shrimper, just the style they'd have in *Swallows and Amazons*; I feel it lends a note of romance and adventure to my task.

Naturally I want Ella to be with me at this pivotal moment. After all, she has been at my side for almost every other significant event in my adult life. It is only fitting, too, because she introduced me to Alizée in the first place.

She wears her own little life jacket and finds herself a comfy spot on the boat so she can witness the crucial exchange at leisure. I've become so used to having her moral support, and with her head resting in my lap, I know I will be bold enough to ask the question.

I give her ears a tickle. She makes me feel that little bit more confident about talking to the man who will (hopefully) be my future father-in-law.

We push off from the jetty and into the loch with all the intent of an intrepid trio on a vital mission. But Jean Gabriel looks perplexed. 'Isn't the mooring buoy over there?' he asks, pointing in the opposite direction.

He's right. I'm floored. I don't know what to say. My mind is churning wildly. We get to the middle of the loch, and I blurt: 'The reason I wanted to get you out on your own was not to moor the boat but to see if it might be possible to ask for your daughter's hand in marriage.'

I babble on, sounding like some incoherent contestant in a cheesy reality show: 'We've come on a long journey together since we met and we make each other very happy, and I would put her first for ever if you would agree.'

Ella, by my side, is willing me on, adopting her best imploring look.

Jean Gabriel looks at us both with an amused smile on his face. 'Are you sure?' he says in his wry Gallic way. 'Do you really know what you're letting yourself in for?'

I gabble back that I'm absolutely sure, and he smiles again and says, 'Well in that case I'd be absolutely delighted to give you my blessing.'

I can still remember my relieved exhalation and the huge smile that bursts across my face. 'But do you mind keeping this quiet,' I insist. 'Just until I find the right moment to ask Alizée.'

Jean Gabriel says: 'Of course. But please can I just tell Laurence, because I've never been able to keep a secret from my wife.'

So the happy deal is sealed. I have managed to stash some Affric Trail Whisky on the boat with two glasses, so I pour us both a small tot of the peaty elixir and Jean Gabriel jokes: 'I'm going to need a bit more than that.' Then we both sit there in the boat marooned needlessly in the middle of the loch, chatting amiably.

A few drinks later, we're ready to go back to the lodge, so we make for the shore. Only then do I realise that we haven't done what we ostensibly set out to do. Alizée – now standing on the edge of the loch – calls to us, perplexed: 'What on earth are you guys doing? You've been out there an hour and the boat is still not on its mooring.'

I'm improvising some inane excuse when Jean Gabriel stands up and gets hold of the boom, which he intends to hold to stabilise himself as he gets out of the boat.

Just as he does so, the cleat holding it suddenly unjams and the boom swings round with him still clinging to it, so his body is suspended perilously over the water while his feet remain rooted to the deck of the boat.

Fortunately he is laughing. I am, too, with relief. 'That was only supposed to happen if you'd said no, then I was going to suspend you there until you changed your mind,' I tell him.

Everything I do with Alizée – every new experience we share – confirms my conviction that I want to spend the rest of my life with her. All I have to do now is to find the right moment to propose.

A couple of weeks later, we go out to spend a few days with her parents at their old water mill near Limoges, a place where Alizée has spent so many happy childhood holidays.

It has an ancient bread oven in an old barn, which they still use. Each morning the enticing smell of newly baked bread lures me out of bed. Wonderful stews in huge earthenware pots simmer quietly in the oven all day while we go out for walks.

We come back to the aromas of slow-cooked cassoulet, lamb tagine, all kinds of casseroles. The meat, always tender, falls off the bone; the gravy is rich and warming.

Jean Gabriel, knowing that I am practical (and perhaps to test the capability of his future son-in-law), sets me tasks fixing all the things that need mending. I patch up the wood burner, repair the water pump, find the right parts to get the tractor running again.

By now you know me well: I love nothing better than restoring mechanical things.

I meet a lot of Alizée's extended family, too, who arrive for lunch during the weekend.

Seeing her with her relatives and in her element – a country girl rather than a townie – confirms that I want her to be in my life for ever. And she has the most wonderful, all-embracing family. It feels like perfection. I try to think of a single thing that jars or feels wrong. There is nothing – although I do lament the fact that I need to brush up considerably on my French.

This, I know, will not come easily to me. In fact I'd much prefer to fix every mechanical item the family owns than revive my rusty, gaffe-prone Franglais and polish it into an acceptable version.

While we're there, Jean Gabriel casts me the occasional knowing glance. We're on our own, I'm stoking the fire and he asks: 'Are you going to do it this weekend, then?' I look at him quizzically.

He clarifies: 'You know, pop the question. You haven't gone off the idea, have you?'

I assure him I haven't, that it's still my intention; I just haven't found the right moment.

We get back home to London and I still haven't done it. I know I'll have to steel myself. Even though I am certain, I worry that she will crush my dreams and tell me there's nothing she wants to do less than marry me.

Anxiety makes me nervous, irrational.

I decide the only thing for it is to grasp the nettle. It must be done. I've never been more sure about any decision in my life. And where better to propose than in the Lake District, where we first started to fall for each other?

I don't want to delay, but the next hurdle is trying to convince Alizée to come with me on the next weekend we're both free. I've bought the perfect antique ring. Ella came with me on the trip to the jeweller's, playing her part in this vital task.

So I suggest to Alizée that we make a trip to the Lakes, specifying the following weekend.

She looks at the weather forecast and sees there are amber storm warnings for the north-west that weekend, while the south will be balmy and sunny.

'Why on earth do you want to drive all the way up there in a rain storm if it's going to be lovely down here?' she asks reasonably.

I assure her I am quite adamant: I want to go whatever the weather. She thinks that I'm joking, barking mad. The more she resists, the more insistent I become. 'I'll pack my bag so I'm all ready when you get home from work on Friday,' I announce.

Friday rolls around. My bag is ready and stowed in the car; the ring and a bottle of champagne are secreted in my rucksack. I've hidden the ring in a dog poo bag, just in case Alizée goes rummaging around in there.

The dogs are eager for the trip, and a plan for the proposal is formed in my mind: we'll go on our favourite walk, the sun will burst through the clouds, I'll find a private spot, uncork the champagne and ask her to be my wife.

Alizée arrives home, checks the forecast. Still lashing rain. 'Are you ready?' I chirp. 'Definitely not,' she says.

I dig my heels in. 'Well, I'll be leaving with the dogs in half an hour,' I tell her. 'If you don't want to come, have a nice weekend and I'll see you on Sunday.'

She can't understand my intransigence. Why won't I see reason and choose a weekend when the weather's better? But I won't budge. I get into the car and – irrationally, ludicrously – decide to set off without her on the weekend I've earmarked to propose to her.

I've driven just a few miles when my mobile rings. It's Alizée. 'Look, I don't want to go tonight. I'm tired. But let's get up early and go tomorrow morning, eh?'

So reluctantly I drive back, unload the dogs, haul my bag and rucksack into the house and set the alarm for 5 a.m.

It is well before dawn as I load the car again. Alizée, tired and grumpy, decides to sit in the back with the dogs. She sleeps for the entire journey and I have the windscreen wipers on full speed as the rain lashes down. The louring skies darken the further north we go.

We arrive at our family's cottage at breakfast time and I spot a brief respite from the rain so propose a walk, but it is still too windy to trek the high fells that we love. I haven't made an exact plan – I decide to ad lib – so we trudge along, the precious ring and champagne stowed in my rucksack, but the right moment does not present itself.

We have a little plunge in a pool on the way home, then we're back in the cottage, the fire is lit and we're cosy as we eat a chicken pie for supper and go early to bed.

Even though I am tired, I lie awake, my mind whirring: I have one day left. I've given myself the weekend; my self-imposed ultimatum. I have to propose to Alizée by Sunday evening.

Sunday dawns. The wind has blown the storm through, but it is still blustery; a grey autumnal day. I make sandwiches for today's walk, check the poo bag with its precious contents, stow our packed lunch next to the tepid champagne in my rucksack.

We set off, following the route of the first walk we ever did together in the Lakes; a nostalgic journey. All the way I'm looking for the optimum moment. We reach the brow of a steep ridge. Here? No, we're too out of breath. Then we're on the summit of the hill. Too windy, too cold.

We start our descent. There's a little nook just off the path, but someone is already there. We stop to eat our sandwiches. Every time I draw breath to speak, a fellow hiker comes into view waving a cheery greeting.

By now I think Alizée must have noticed my awkwardness. Even as we eat our lunch I clutch the rucksack jealously, not even allowing her to take out her bottle of water. When I go off for a pee behind a rock, I take it with me. Does she think I'm being really weird? Certainly I think I am.

Every time in the past when I've tried to broach the subject of our future together, she's been mildly dismissive, telling me she's not yet ready for marriage. 'How will you know when you're ready?', I pressed her.

'I guess you just feel it,' she shrugged.

So now that I'm confronted with asking her outright, I'm fraught, anxious; wondering whether I've entirely misjudged her mood.

We arrive back at the cottage, the elation I hoped for dampened into quiet resignation. We only have a few hours left in the Lakes. Soon we will need to pack for home. On Monday the routines of work will resume; the romance I tried to conjure will ebb away.

'Let's just pop down for one last quick swim in the river,' I suggest.

Alizée agrees. So off we go, with Ella – and, of course, the rucksack.

As we jump into the water, the sun comes out – a burst of radiance – and we splash around for a couple of minutes before leaping out.

Now! I tell myself as we scramble onto the bank, and my words come out, an unintelligible jumble, interrupting Alizée, who is talking about her work plans for next week.

'I've just got something to do, to say, to you, for us,' I ramble incoherently as she looks at me, perplexed. Then I blurt: 'Will you do me the greatest honour of marrying me?'

Chapter Twelve

A Highland Loch-down . . . and a Home of Our Own

———

Alizée looks at me, genuinely shocked. Clearly this is the last thing she was expecting. For a split second I wonder if my world is about to crumble.

A brief vision of her standing there, stunned, against a backdrop of inquisitive Herdwick sheep stays with me.

Then she cries, 'Yes!' and there are tears. She puts on the ring. We have a cuddle and a little cry together. All the pent-up nervousness that has made me irritable and jittery for days evaporates.

I look across at Ella, curled up on the rucksack. I've practised saying the words to her in moments when we were alone. 'Will you marry me?' Then, 'Will you do me the honour of marrying me?' She's heard the phrases many times.

Now, as Alizée and I hug and cry and skip around, Ella joins us for a little victory dance, jumping and wagging her tail. She shares our elation. I like to think she knows why we are happy, and I tell her that she'll soon officially have a mum to share her care.

We race back to the cottage for a cup of tea and eat up the cheese that is left from our weekend's food rations. A modest feast to celebrate our engagement. Then it occurs to me that I've lugged a bottle of champagne over three fells and we haven't had a single sip of it.

It is too late to open it now – I won't have a drink if I'm driving – so we both laugh about the fact that the effort expended in hiding it for two days was wasted.

Looking back now, I think this was the most nerve-racking moment of my life. How many men, over the centuries, have uttered the words 'Will you marry me?' and been rebuffed? I cannot imagine how bereft they must have been.

But for Alizée and me everything now feels bathed in a glow of happiness. On the drive home I reach out occasionally to hold her hand. The dogs are snoring audibly on the seat behind us, and we are chatting so animatedly we forget to phone anyone and tell them our news.

Back in London it doesn't feel as if we've only been away for 48 hours. Over the next few days there are lots of excited FaceTimes and phone calls to the family.

'Guess what?' we say.

'You've bought a house?' they hazard.

Nobody guesses correctly. And then comes the revelation – and everyone is delighted.

Three months post engagement pass in a whirl. Ella accompanies me on the red carpet at the *GQ* Man of the Year awards – I think

I'm the first invitee to ask if I can bring my dog – then Alizée and I prepare for a wonderful French family Christmas; our first together since we got engaged.

I now feel firmly embedded in her warm and welcoming family, and once again we go to her grandparents' chalet in the Alps for New Year. This has such happy memories for her, because when her parents were travelling the world with the diplomatic service, the chalet was always a stable base camp; the haven she came to for holidays.

Now we revisit the places she has always loved: the pristine snowfields, the ski slopes, each one a piece of the jigsaw that is Alizée.

But it is late 2019 and the world is already murmuring about a respiratory infection coming out of Wuhan in China: COVID. There are, as yet, no travel restrictions, but when we come home in January, our buoyant mood deflates. There is an eviction notice on the doormat.

The owner of the house we have rented is giving us three months' notice that he is selling. He wants his house back. We need to find a new place to live.

We're disconsolate. We love Battersea and don't want to leave, but this gives us fresh impetus to start looking for a house to buy together.

We put our wedding plans on hold temporarily, and because we enjoy our proximity to the park, where the dogs can exercise before we go to work each day, we decide to search for a place nearby.

We find a wonderful 'doer-upper', shabby and down-at-heel, but the challenge is getting a mortgage.

And COVID is taking hold. We're heading for lockdown and the owner of the house we've rented takes his house off the market when his buyer drops out, meaning we could stay. But the whole country is in a state of restless unease and, like others, we're craving a sense of stability. As we're casting around for a place to stay, my parents remind us that they have plenty of room at Bucklebury and we're welcome there. It is a lovely offer: the stability and comfort of Mum and Dad's is, we all agree, the best temporary solution. Next day we start packing our boxes and bags to go and stay with them.

So once again I'm at Bucklebury – this time with my new fiancée – and the dogs are delighted they are back in the countryside.

As if life isn't busy enough, during this time we decide that Luna is ready to have her first batch of puppies on her next season and the hunt is on for a boyfriend for her.

We come across the perfect match, but the meeting is put on hold until the time is right – which just happens to be soon after we arrive at Mum and Dad's.

Social distancing makes it tricky to mate the dogs, but I manage to hold both Luna and her boyfriend quite efficiently while they get on with their business. Eight weeks later, she has a litter of six puppies, which takes the dog tally at Bucklebury up to twelve.

Dad smiles ruefully and remarks on the ratio of dogs to humans in the house, so I set about assigning the pups to their new homes. Catherine has earmarked one to replace their beloved Lupo – their wedding gift from me – who died, aged eight, in 2020.

I decide to donate the proceeds from selling the rest of the pups to Pets As Therapy, knowing as I do so keenly how vital their work is.

I am sharply conscious that in lockdown many people will be acquiring dogs in the optimistic – but misplaced – belief that they will still be able to look after them properly once they go back to work.

Anticipating the number that will need to be rehomed, I decide to try to help with some online training tips. (Obedient dogs are, after all, much easier to care for.)

I post instructions on how to train your dog to sit and stay, to walk to heel, to lie down, to go to bed. I also offer practical advice on trimming nails, cleaning teeth, removing ticks. The favourable response from owners is overwhelming.

As COVID continues to grip, and as other people indulge in making banana bread and sourdough starters, I find old passions coming to the fore. As you know, I have a soft heart for injured animals too, and when a local farmer tells me he has a blind lamb, I offer to adopt it.

Next time my dear parents come down for breakfast, I am bottle-feeding the tiny newcomer at the kitchen table. My father rubs his eyes in disbelief. 'What next, James?' he sighs.

The lamb spends all his time with the dogs and adopts their habits. They embrace him as one of their family. He walks on a lead with me, and because he enjoys trotting round the garden, we name him Captain, after Captain Tom Moore.

Bit by bit, we realise that Captain is starting to see things. The blindness that afflicted him at birth is slowly resolving itself. He is beginning to enjoy sighted life, kicking his legs and frolicking as the dogs run alongside him.

He comes to my whistle; like the dogs, he walks to heel. He is a source of pride and joy, the pet lamb that follows me everywhere.

There is something about lockdown – perhaps the slower pace of life and my proximity to nature – that revives all my childhood instincts for caring for sick animals.

One day a domesticated brown rabbit arrives in the garden at Bucklebury. I'm concerned that the dogs will worry him, so I set a humane trap to catch him and put posters round the village with his photo: 'Does anyone recognise this rabbit?'

No one claims him so I adopt him and name him Pretzel after his colouring. He, in turn, falls in love with the youngest of my dog family, Nala, who is Ella's granddaughter and Zulu's daughter. Nala loves Pretzel back. It is almost as if they are kin. He also takes to my chickens and decides to nest with them overnight.

Every morning when I go to collect the eggs, out pops Pretzel and a fluttering clutch of hens, who also appear to enjoy his company.

Meanwhile Captain is now a fully grown sheep and Dad asks: 'How long is he staying?'

'I have a plan,' I assure him, not even certain myself what the plan is.

A bit later, when restrictions temporarily loosen, close friends ask us to join their sailing trip in a 1930s gaff-rig schooner, *Puritan*. It is a grand old rig that was used as a patrol boat by the US Navy during World War II, tracking submarines by stealth, having been sold to them for $1 by its previous owner.

We sail out to the Ionian Sea to an island called Stromboli, which has an active volcano. We go ashore and have a wonderful dinner. Simple but delicious: fish, caught that morning and glistening fresh from the sea, seasoned and fried in olive oil. Afterwards we come back into the cockpit and chat about our wedding plans.

Then someone remarks: 'Did you know a ship's captain can perform a marriage at sea?'

In fact there are lots of provisos – the captain has to be legally qualified as a notary or justice of the peace (an unlikely eventuality), unless he and the couple just happen to be Japanese – but the idea starts a flight of fancy.

Alizée says: 'If the volcano erupts while we're here, we'll get married.' Everyone laughs and agrees.

Suddenly there is an almighty flash, billowing clouds and a flow of molten lava from Stromboli. We all gasp. What we don't realise is that this volcano is one of the most active in the world. It erupts almost every day, but mostly at night.

Alizée scuttles off down below: she has no intention of getting married without our families and friends with us. 'And Ella has to be there,' she adds as she disappears. I nod. Of course she does.

When we return home, the winter of 2020 is approaching. Another lockdown threatens and we offer to go to Glen Affric to help look after the estate. We drive up with the dogs, loading the car with supplies at Beauly, a beautiful Scottish town with an ancient priory. An hour's drive away, it is the nearest town to the remote Highland outpost where we are staying.

We do not know when we set off that we will be there for a couple of months due to the prolonged pandemic restrictions, working from our temporary home, a little cottage by the loch. We settle into the quiet rhythm of our routine, working in the week, then taking off on adventures at the weekend.

We decide to go Munro-bagging, climbing as many Munros as we can while we are there. (Munros are mountains of more than 3,000 feet, and bagging means reaching the summit.) We set off on brisk winter Saturdays, the dogs racing ahead of us, a packed lunch stowed in our backpack, and climb.

We sail and paddleboard on the loch – the dogs joining us too – into sunsets so stunning they bathe the whole glen in rosy light.

Feeding the horses, Rosco, Menno and Marcus, has become a happy daily ritual. The dogs trot behind us as we drive the quad bike, laden with hay bales, to the field where they're waiting, frisky with anticipation, for their fodder.

They nuzzle the dogs, who dart and gambol with them, excited by the sudden flurry of activity.

The great Lakeland walker and writer Alfred Wainwright once observed: 'There's no such thing as bad weather, only unsuitable clothing,' and this adage could not apply more keenly than in the Highlands. But Alizée and I, dressed in woollens and waterproofs, are never perturbed by the cold or wet. Driving polar winds and horizontal rain do not deter us from our 20-kilometre hikes and runs.

One weekend we lace up our fell-running trainers and resolve to race to the top of the nearby peak. It is lonely, rugged and challenging; there is no path, but we follow a series of little cairns (rock piles), the dogs, excited, scampering alongside us.

The wind has a sharp edge, and drenching icy rain whips up as we begin the ascent. Sleet stings our cheeks like needles, and on one wind-lashed ledge Alizée can barely stand. We almost make it – we are within metres of the peak – when the cold and wet of the gathering dusk defeats us and we turn tail to skip and leap our way downhill again.

There's a fisherman's bothy two miles from our cottage, where we stop to light a fire and, in the steamy heat, revive ourselves before the final leg of our run.

Sometimes I think that Alizée, despite her slender frame, is tougher than me. She never baulks at challenges; in fact she seems to relish them.

The bothy is a regular stop on our runs and walks, and we have stashed some supplies there so we can light a fire and eat in its cosy glow. Often we take a shortcut back to the cottage from there, crossing the loch in a little boat moored at the water's edge.

After one long weekend walk, we find that the loch waters have dropped and the boat has run aground. Even with our combined strength we cannot shift it, so we have to trek the final two miles round the edge of the loch in the moonlight.

We have a hip flask full of whisky – the Glen Affric I drank with Alizée's father – and we get slightly merry as we march along, singing at the tops of our voices, arriving at the welcome haven of the cottage to a steamy bath.

As we are in lockdown, we notice even more the intensity of the silence. We find time to sit quietly observing the natural world, busy around us. A nervous vole scuttles for cover. There are hares boxing, ptarmigan with their snow-white winter plumage preening on the rocks, plump as partridges. Eagles swoop and dive, and before the coldest months of the winter set in, we spot ospreys lunging into the loch for their fish dinners.

Around every corner there is something of heart-stopping beauty. Even the lichen that colonises the pines – it is called old man's beard – seems invested with a special, ethereal magic.

It is almost as if the trees talk to each other, their branches rustling in the wind. The moment you pass, they fall silent, only to return to their mystical conversation when no one is there to listen.

The special peace of these months teaches us to observe and be grateful, not least for the fact that we have such wonderful walks around us.

I am reminded that you don't need to get on a plane or a boat to have an adventure. They are right here on your doorstep if you look for them, in meadows, parks and muddy lanes; on windswept commons and hilltops. All you need to reach them is a brave heart, waterproofs and a sturdy pair of boots.

One enchanted morning, we wake to find that five inches of snow has fallen. When we step outside, the quiet has an almost tangible quality. This is a silence so deep it is impenetrable. No distant hum of traffic. No planes. We decide to climb another Munro and set off rugged up like Michelin men, the only noise the squeak of our boots through the snow on pathways untrodden.

Back at the cottage in the evening, we light a fire outside in the fire pit, lie on our backs and count the stars.

Next day, in the soft grey dawn, we sip our morning tea by the edge of the loch before our regular morning dip.

A low mist hangs over the mountains; there is the promise of a golden winter's day ahead. We gird ourselves for the leap, then jump. And as we duck our heads under the water, we shiver and laugh.

The dogs join us, of course – Ella, Inka, Luna and Mabel – swimming with their noses above the waterline. We strike out into the freezing depths for just a few metres, then it's time to swim back to the shoreline, shake ourselves off and rush into the cottage to shower.

Back inside, the dogs are snug in their little turquoise towelling coats; Alizée and I are cosy in jumpers, thick trousers and stout boots. A wood fire blazes.

Thoughts turn to breakfast: porridge with honey from my bees, then new-laid eggs and my home-made sourdough bread.

We have no mobile phone reception, so our main means of communication with the outside world – aside from emails – is the house landline. It has only rung a couple of times in all the weeks we've been there.

It rings again today, the unexpectedness of it startling. It's Mum, and she's excited.

'Guess what?'

'I've no idea,' I say, wondering what is so urgent.

'A farm in the village next to us is coming onto the market, and it would be ideal for you and Alizée,' she says.

My heart does a little dance of joy. What could be better than a house of our own in the country – and so near to Mum and Dad? What's more, we know the family who own it: I went to school with their granddaughter. It seems a heaven-sent opportunity, and because properties in the country are selling fast, we know we need to get back to Berkshire at once to view it.

Christmas is approaching and the government has given us permission to see our families, so we arrange to drive down from

Scotland the next day. There is social distancing. Windows will be open, masks worn, but we can view the house.

When we walk inside, we fall instantly in love. It is a slightly ramshackle sixteenth-century cottage, its oldest part built in the reign of Henry VIII with all sorts of little extensions added over the years. There are leaded casement windows, creaking wooden floors, inglenook fireplaces and ancient beams so low I'd graze my head if I didn't duck.

It was last modernised, I imagine, 50 or so years ago, but we are undeterred by the avocado and peach bathroom suites and already our imaginations are taking flight. There is land too – fields and woods – on which we can keep the flock of Herdwick sheep we have dreamed of. Captain can come too.

The 70-year-old tractor Dad gave me for my 18th birthday can at last be put to use on our own land. We begin to dream about the adventure awaiting us.

During our viewing, Ella quickly makes herself at home. She finds a dark little nook where the bricks are warm from the heat of the wood-burning stove, snuggles down there and falls asleep.

For a few minutes we can't find her – has she wandered off on an adventure? – then we see her snoozing peacefully and take it as an omen. If she feels comfortable enough to sleep in a spot she has chosen for herself, she obviously likes the house too.

There are so many reasons why it feels right. Alizée gets on well with Mum and Dad – she has no qualms at all about living so close to her future in-laws – and they love her too.

The village has two pubs and there are another seven or so within walking distance. We laugh about the fantastic pub crawls we'll have.

We're so excited. Although we love Battersea, our long-term aim was to buy a little farm in the country. We've just got there far sooner than we could have dared to hope. So our decision is made instantly. Between Christmas and New Year, we put in an offer.

I am at the vet's picking up tick and flea treatment for the dogs when I get the call: 'Your offer has been accepted.' I rush home to tell Alizée, my excitement only slightly clouded by the fact that we now have the weighty responsibility of securing our first mortgage.

The house is tenanted and we know it will be six months before the tenants move out and we can move in. We can barely wait until June 2021, when we can start to make our mark on our first home.

Our heads are still buzzing with happy plans when in February, not long after we have exchanged contracts, devastating news reaches us. Alizée's adored dad has died suddenly on a bike ride, from a cardiac arrest.

We can hardly take in the scope and scale of the tragedy. He was a fit man, only 61, who loved to cycle in the hills above the Côte d'Azur in the south of France where he and Laurence had a house in Bormes-les-Mimosas.

He was within metres of their home when he died, a man of such charm, humour and erudition who welcomed me so warmly into his family. And now he has gone, it is as if a light has gone out in Alizée's life.

We are so close to getting married, and now her dad will never see her as a bride or give her away. She is broken, inconsolable.

As a form of distraction, we try to throw ourselves into our wedding plans. Alizée knows she wants to get married in Bormes-les-Mimosas, the medieval town her parents loved, where they had decided to settle for their retirement, and we set a date in September at the town hall there; the mayor is to marry us in front of just 40 family and friends because COVID restrictions still apply.

Meanwhile, Alizée busies herself with visits to our new house, and with the permission of the tenants, we turn the soil in the vegetable garden and sow early seeds to prepare for the spring. There is comfort in these rituals of growth and renewal, in the slow and patient toil of gardening.

Back and forth Alizée goes to France to see her mum, and I go with her to her parents' home, Le Moulin at Limoges, where Laurence is starting to sift through the memorabilia of lives richly lived.

Driving back after one trip, we spend a day with Alizée's grandmother en route. She has just turned 94; it is lovely to catch up with her and spend precious time together.

When moving day finally arrives, we rush to get the keys to our first home and there are warm hugs with the owners' daughter, who is delighted we will cherish the little farm as much as her family did.

I have one slightly nervous question. The house is called Skilcroft, after a nearby wood, but we prefer its original, historic name, Hunter's Moon Farm, and I ask if there would be any objection if we changed it back. The hunter's moon is the full moon that comes at the end of October and traditionally provides nocturnal light at the start of the hunting season, when birds and animals are preparing for the long winter ahead and are fattened and meaty, ready for humans to eat.

There is something about the view of the full moon from the house as it rises like a copper disc over the canopy of trees that makes the name seem apt and romantic. Everyone agrees that we should revert to it.

And so we become the proud owners of Hunter's Moon Farm, and the business of unpacking our belongings begins. There are all kinds of heirlooms: pieces of furniture from my grandparents' home that Catherine originally had at St Andrews University then passed on to me; a chair that Dad made; treasures from Alizée's travels and her many childhood homes all over the world.

We struggle to get most of it through the front door, which is just five feet high, so we take out window frames to manoeuvre things into the house, humming and hawing about which items we will keep and what to discard.

Once everything is stowed inside, I rifle through umpteen boxes – regretting that we haven't labelled one of them – to find a corkscrew so we can open a bottle of wine and toast Jean Gabriel. It is a poignant day: our moving-in day marks his birthday, and we're crushed by regret that he won't ever visit us here.

But exploring our new home still holds a frisson of excitement. Peeping underneath the carpets, we discover gnarled old floorboards we cannot wait to expose.

The dogs sniff round. They seem to take to their new home, although they are a bit confused. They've walked past this house often over the years but never spent time here. Only Ella instantly settles in. She has already found her little niche – warmed by the fire in winter and cool in the summer – and because she lies there so comfortably, she helps to settle the other dogs too.

It dawns on us that we now live on a small farm and everything around us is growing as summer sets in. We make plans to start our first grass harvest to make hay.

Tilly, my trusty old tractor, is pressed into service, but because she was built in 1953, I use a newer tractor to cut the grass while Alizée drives Tilly and does the tedding (lifting and turning the grass) to dry it.

We pass each other as we file up and down the fields, Alizée turning a row after I cut it; she beaming up at me as I smile back at her.

The dogs come out with us, and during this glorious golden day they find shady spots to lie in while we work, then rush through the cut grass as we finish the harvest, mad with the simple joy of it.

And I think to myself that I have realised a dream. I'm living in the country on a farm with all my dogs around me, and my wife-to-be at my side.

Chapter Thirteen

To Love and to Cherish

———

Our wedding day – 11 September 2021 – is fast approaching, and because there are still restrictions on the sizes of gatherings, we have to whittle down the numbers. We settle on who we will invite. Family and close friends. Forty maximum.

Neither of us, you will have gathered, is a meticulous forward-planner, but we realise that we can't leave it too late to decide how we are going to celebrate.

We've already spent time exploring the beaches and coves of the stretch of the Côte d'Azur around Bormes-les-Mimosas, and on one visit we stumble across a little restaurant on the beach, Café Leoube.

We ask (careful not to let the cat out of the bag) if they do parties, and an accommodating chap called Jerome tells us with a knowing smile that he can fit us in on the very date we've booked the town hall for the ceremony.

We don't have time to organise official wedding invitations, so we call our guests. Fortunately for us, everyone is delighted to join us in September.

We want them to make the most of their time with us, so decide to host a dinner on the Thursday before the wedding in the beautiful old town, with its cobbled streets and cascades of bougainvillea.

Our wedding meal is to be venison from Glen Affric, because the place has a special resonance: that was where I asked Alizée's dad for her hand in marriage.

Back in London, I'm hastily considering what to wear. The thought of getting married in a morning coat in the sweltering heat of the south of France isn't appealing, so the hunt is on for a nice lightweight suit.

Ella and I pop into Ralph Lauren – where they're dog-friendly – and I spot a linen suit that looks just right. I'm nervous about saying the word 'wedding', just in case our secret slips out, so I just try on a couple of suits while Ella looks on, and take some photos of both of us to show to Alizée. If she approves, I'll get her to come to the shop to help me choose one.

Meanwhile, I realise that Alizée has said nothing to me about her dress. I know, of course, that traditionally it is kept a closely guarded secret until the big day. But there hasn't been a whisper about a shopping trip, no conferring with friends; not even the slightest murmur, suggestion or clue.

'Have you sorted your dress?' I ask her, because the silence has become unsettling.

'Oh yes. All sorted,' she replies, sounding almost blasé.

The next week I make an appointment at Ralph Lauren. Ella, Alizée and her mum come with me, and we settle between us on a cream linen suit and a blue shirt; the shirt a little daring, as I'm aware that sweat patches will be more visible with a light colour.

Next we sort out Ella and Mabel's passports and get all the requisite health checks, because they are going to be our flower girls; their role – which I know they'll fulfil wonderfully – is to warmly welcome every guest.

Barely a week before the wedding, I have a meeting with the people who manufacture dog food for my company. Sales have been increasing; all seems to be going well. But as soon as I walk into the room, I detect unease.

Right at the start of the meeting they tell me: 'We're sorry to be delivering bad news, but we're unable to supply your food any longer.' They simply cannot keep up with demand.

There is only three months' worth of dog food in reserve, which makes me feel anxious. The next morning I'm due to drive to the south of France to finalise arrangements for the wedding. All the way down I'm thinking of a plan that will have to be executed as soon as I return.

But once I arrive at Bormes-les-Mimosas, I'm in wedding mode and switch off those concerns. As well as the official celebrations, I've also booked a restaurant for supper for the day before to break the ice, so the French side of the family can get to know the English side and vice versa and the wedding day itself will be more relaxed.

When we got engaged, Jean Gabriel and Laurence offered us a white Citroën 2CV for our wedding car. The iconic little French car, first manufactured in 1948, has ingenious suspension. It was designed to cross a freshly ploughed field without breaking a basket of eggs on the passenger seat. The lack of paved roads in France at the time made this a useful selling point.

We're thrilled to have this classic car – with an open top – for our wedding, delighted that we'll make our first journey as man and wife over the cobbled streets of Bormes-les-Mimosas not in some flashy chauffeur-driven limousine, but in an unpretentious 2CV.

Our friends have already commandeered it to decorate it.

Guests start to arrive on the Wednesday before our big day, but Alizée and I have not yet done our table plan. It is more complicated than most, as some guests speak only French, others just English, and we need to make sure nobody is cut adrift without someone to talk to.

But there are so many calls on our time and attention we forget entirely about the plan. Thursday's meal is a wonderful warm-up, then on Friday we rent 25 bicycles and invite friends and family to re-create Jean Gabriel's last cycle ride.

Alizée makes a last-minute dash to the boulangerie and, with just half an hour to spare, orders cheese and ham baguettes for everyone's lunch. The bakery goes into a frenzy of slicing and spreading, and miraculously they are ready in time.

We retrace Jean Gabriel's route along the meandering clifftops with their sparkling ocean views; we take in the lingering scent of the last wild lavender. It is a nature trail; the air is heady with pine as well as flowers, and crickets chirrup. We keep an eye out for wild boars, and cycle steadily in the warm, dry heat, wary of bruising or grazing our legs before the big day. For Alizée it is bittersweet, conjuring mixed emotions: the sadness of loss and longing, but joy, too, that her papa's last journey was one of such sublime beauty.

At the end we swim, reminisce, laugh, cry and eat baguettes. It is our own small, impromptu memorial to Jean Gabriel. We are glad to honour him.

Then there is a boules match – France v England – and we drink pastis before we get ready for another evening out.

My mum and dad and Pippa and James all join us for the cycle ride, but Catherine, William and their children are not due to come until the morning of our wedding.

To our huge surprise and delight, however, they arrive on Friday evening, earlier than planned, to join in the pre-wedding meal.

We want them to be able to relax without fear of intrusion, and it is challenging because the restaurant where we eat is quite exposed. But – thanks in part to our low-key, last-minute plans – no paparazzi find us.

Alizée and I had agreed that we'd be in bed no later than 11 p.m., but at 1 a.m. I have to be dragged off the dance floor at the beach café. We stagger back to our little seaside villa, where the dogs are waiting for us, and dutifully sleep in different rooms, setting early alarms.

As I drift into sleep, I'm jolted awake by a sudden urgent thought. 'Oh God! The table plan!'

Memo to self: put it to the top of the to-do list tomorrow morning.

With that thought, I nuzzle Ella, who is sleeping at the end of my bed, and before I know it, it's morning and my wedding-day alarm is ringing shrill in my ear.

Drawing back the curtains to a glittering, sunny day, I wish I'd gone to bed earlier, but the sea beckons and I know a dip will revive me. Alizée and I run down to the jetty and jump into the water. There is a splosh as Mabel launches herself in after us, while Ella swims more demurely in the shallows.

Our heads cleared, we are ready for our breakfast of croissants and scrambled egg. Then the table plan! Hastily we assemble our thoughts, agree to send them to the team at Café Léoube, then promptly forget as the day's excitement ramps up.

Alizée's bridesmaids arrive in a babble of chatter, and it's time for me to leave and meet my groomsmen, who have organised (another) breakfast. They all look a little bit the worse for wear.

After I went to bed, they stayed out drinking, but a couple of Bloody Marys each seems to fix them, and two hours pass in amiable chat before we realise it's about time we all got ready.

When I pop back to our villa to pick up Mabel and Ella and get changed, one of Alizée's bridesmaids intercepts me.

'No need at all to worry,' she says, sounding distinctly worried, 'but do you happen to know where Alizée's dress is? No one seems to know.' She looks distraught.

The plan was to keep the dress lying flat, she tells me, but I wonder if someone has accidentally hung it in a cupboard. A series of frantic phone calls later, it emerges that the dress has been whisked away and steamed and is now ready for Alizée to wear.

Amid all the commotion, one person is blissfully unconcerned. Alizée says calmly, 'If no one can find it, it doesn't matter. I'll just wear something else.'

All is now running to schedule. The 2CV and Alizée's grandfather are waiting to take her to the *mairie* (town hall). I make my way there as the mayor is welcoming friends and family.

A light breeze riffles through the room from open windows with views over the tumbling rooftops of the old town to the bay. I stop to reflect on how happy I am – trying to freeze-frame this moment in my mind – with my family and Alizée's around me, so many of those I love close to me.

I blink away a tear, and Ella, ever sensitive to the subtle shifts in my mood, comes to gently prod my hand and settle me.

Ella and Mabel both have gauze bows round their necks and have been dutifully – and delightedly – welcoming everyone to the town hall.

Suddenly their ears register movement outside. Alizée and her grandfather have arrived, just ten minutes late. Mabel, Ella and I keep our gazes fixed ahead. Only the thudding of Mabel's wagging tail, which is hitting a nearby chair, breaks the tense and excited silence.

The music starts, and I turn to catch a glimpse of Alizée starting to walk towards me, her eyes sparkling, her corn-coloured hair half circling her head, half flowing loose. She wears a dress with an embroidered handkerchief hem that fits her slim frame perfectly.

I do not realise it at the time, but it is my mum's wedding dress, last worn when she got married to Dad 41 years earlier.

Neither do I know – yet – the story of how Alizée comes to be wearing it now, but I learn later that she and Mum were clearing out cupboards together at Bucklebury during lockdown when Mum came across the dress.

They talked about it and Mum asked Alizée if she'd like to try it on. She did – and it fitted her as if it had been made for her. Mum asked her if she'd like to wear it on her wedding day, and Alizée said she could think of nothing better.

A few small adjustments were made so she could wear it off the shoulder. And here she is now, a bouquet of wild flowers in her hand, walking towards me. I feel as if the love surrounding me is palpable.

I clear my throat, blink away tears and the ceremony begins. My dear friend Mike reads my favourite poem, 'What I Learned about Love, I Learned from my Dog'. Nick is our ring-bearer. Laurence makes a short speech.

I only have a few words to speak, but I cannot hold back the tears. By now there is not a dry eye in the room.

The wedding ceremony passes in a blur of happiness. Documents are witnessed and signed, photos taken, and before I know it we are outside in the sunshine where the 2CV is waiting, walking through a hail of lavender confetti, then jumping into the car and driving off with tin cans rattling behind us.

We make our way through the old streets to Léoube, where everyone will join us for lunch and a party on the beach. Ella and Mabel are sitting on the back seat, a light breeze cools us through the open roof, music plays, horns toot, well-wishers wave. It is a magical ten-minute drive and I never want it to end.

At the beach there are canapés and rosé wine from the vineyard next door, and Jerome comes up to greet me with a bear hug. 'James, is there any update on the table plan?' he asks tentatively. OMG. We're due to eat in ten minutes.

All I have is a photo on my phone of the hastily sketched plan Alizée and I made this morning. I send it to Jerome. He only just has time to marshal everyone into the seats we have chosen for them before the meal is served.

We sit down to eat with our feet in the sand and the dappled sunlight on our heads. There is a buzz of conversation and laughter. Everyone has someone to talk to. Everyone is relaxed and happy. The only sadness is Jean Gabriel's absence.

I stand to make my speech and I'm feeling nervous, particularly as part of it will be in French, and my linguistic skills combined with my dyslexia make this a potential minefield.

'*Accueil*', or 'welcome', is what I'm supposed to say.

'*Enculé*', or 'b***er', is what I actually say.

The entire French contingent of guests erupts into laughter. Thinking everything is going far better than I anticipated, I plough on, enjoying the riotous reception.

Even so, I feel more secure once my speech has segued into English. I thank my parents for all they have done for me, and express the hope that one day I will follow their model when I raise my own children.

I look across at my sisters, smiling at me, and thank them for all their love and support. Then I tell them I think I've let them off lightly. I will not be asking them to do their flute duet.

There is no formality; no one stands on ceremony. My six nieces and nephews run round, crawling between people's legs. Mabel has dived into the sea. Alizée smiles and whispers to me, 'I wish I could do that, too.' Then Mabel comes back from her swim and shakes herself all over us.

Only then does Alizée mention my mispronunciation – and happily, by then I am too elated to be worried.

It has been a tiring day for Mabel and Ella. They've welcomed our guests, stood at our sides throughout the ceremony and stayed with us during our meal; supported us in the way only they know how, unobtrusively and loyally.

Now they need a nap, so I settle them into the back of the 2CV with the roof open to the sky and a gentle breeze to cool them, and they sleep after their long, happy day.

Then the music is turned up and the beach becomes a dance floor. Alizée and I have not prepared a first dance, but everyone is encouraging us to do one. Typically I muddle the whole thing up, asking the DJ to put on a record, then – obviously something has been lost in translation – going to the loo the minute it comes on.

He tries again. This time I'm checking the dogs when our song begins. Finally, third time lucky, Queen's hit 'Don't Stop Me Now' rings out when I'm actually there, and Alizée and I find ourselves in the middle of a whirling circle of friends and family, all dancing around us.

Everyone is smiling and laughing and I couldn't be happier. I want to capture this moment and keep it for ever; two minutes of simple, unalloyed joy in a day of pure bliss.

The sun is coming up when we leave for our little villa by the sea, and we cannot close our eyes to sleep before we have run to the jetty again and jumped into the sea. So we have our last swim of a glorious day, then giggle our way to bed.

The next day there is brunch in the beach café, and then we're off on our mini-moon with friends on a boat that has just come from Saint-Tropez Regatta. The crew could see the lights from our party as they set anchor in the bay the night before.

Alizée and I wade into the sea and a tender boat picks us up for a few magical days on board. The dogs stay with Laurence, not because they don't enjoy sailing, but because we're concerned it will be too hot for them.

After such times of heightened emotions, it sometimes feels anticlimactic to go back home, but we are so excited to return to our little farm, settle in for the winter and make it feel like home.

There is the matter of the dog food manufacturer to resolve, too, and sometimes positive things happen when you give yourself breathing space. It takes a few months, but we seek advice from industry experts and decide to produce the food ourselves in our own kitchens.

My company is now renamed James & Ella to reflect my bond with my beloved dog, and we prepare to expand into retail.

Meanwhile, there are hedges to be cut, vegetable plots to be weeded, logs to be chopped and house renovations to begin.

Not long after we come home, Alizée and I go blackberry-picking with the dogs. There is a clump of them, abundant and glistening black in the autumn sunshine, on our 30-acre plot, just past an avenue of oak trees. This year the harvest is prolific, and as we intend to live off the land as far as we can, we pick the lot to bottle or freeze, to make into compotes and pies.

Ella loves blackberrying. She has mastered the technique of pulling the fruit off the bramble bushes so successfully we have to limit the number she eats. Her tongue has turned blue by the time our baskets are laden and we're ready to go back home.

It is partly because Ella loves them so much – and also because they are good for dogs in the right quantities – that blackberries feature in some of my dog food recipes today.

Every day there is work to do on the farm, and I'm out on the tractor one evening when I crush the end of one of the fingers on my left hand, ripping the nail off and exposing the flesh underneath. Then I notice that a slice of the finger is hanging on by a thread – the bone underneath is visible – so I bind my bloodied hand in a rag to keep all the bits intact and run into the house.

Alizée is squeamish, so I don't show her the finger, but I tell her I need to go to hospital. It's 10 p.m.

'Why?' she asks.

She wants to see the wound, and when I do show her, she almost faints. She's tough but hates the sight of blood, so she is feeling queasy. She comes with me, but because she is still quite unsteady, I drive.

On the way, we spot a man lying slumped and inert by the edge of the road. I stop the car and put the hazard lights on, and we rush to help him. Smelling wafts of alcohol on his breath, we realise why he has passed out and call an ambulance.

Waiting with him until the ambulance arrives delays us further, and it's 1 a.m. before we arrive at A&E in Reading, where I'm bandaged and strapped. An appointment is made for the next day, when I'm to have the chopped-off bit of my finger stitched back on by specialists.

We both laugh at how lucky I am with my timing. Had I mangled my finger a week earlier, I'd have arrived at our wedding with a vast bandage on my left hand and we'd have struggled to get my wedding band on.

We think about how daft it would have looked in the photos – and as if we've summoned it with our thoughts, our wedding album arrives. We open a bottle of wine and sit down together to look at the photos, reliving the day's perfection.

They span all four days of our time in Bormes-les-Mimosas and could not have captured more perfectly the informality and happiness of those days. Both Catherine and Pippa had very formal weddings, and their photos reflect this. But here we all are sitting on hay bales in a field, Catherine and William beaming; Pippa's husband James freeze-framed in profile laughing with one of the kids; Alizée and I in the centre of them all with Mum, Dad and Laurence smiling at our sides; Ella and Mabel revelling in the fun.

We go through them all. Memories are revived. Moments we missed in the happy blur of the day are immortalised.

We asked the guests not to take photos on their phones because we wanted them to enjoy the moment – and we didn't want our wedding album to feature lots of people taking photos on their phones. So in our album everyone is focusing on having a good time.

And it was all impromptu. We spotted the field and the hay bales close by and thought the rustic setting was exactly right for us. After all, we were cutting hay shortly before we got married and would be every year as the cycles of growth and harvest continued.

We've been looking forward, too, to putting our stamp on our new home, and Alizée decorates the kitchen, painting the solid and serviceable pine units a dark petrol blue and installing rows of Kilner jars full of beans and pulses on the shelves, which she also paints.

We decide that the avocado bath with its matching loo, bidet and sink has to come out, so we resolve to tackle that and give the bathroom an uplift. It is easier said than done.

I go into the attic and find a network of hundred-year-old pipes criss-crossing the small roof space. It takes patient application to isolate the tap that turns off the water before I can rip out the sink, bidet and loo.

The next problem is the cast-iron bath, which is too wide to fit through the tiny bedroom door through which we access the bathroom.

The stairs are also narrow and winding. Even if I could manoeuvre the bath through the door, I'd have trouble getting it down them.

So I decide to take out the window frame and, building a scaffold tower on the outside of the house, lower the vast bath down on a winch.

I'm doing this on my own – coaxing the bath down with help from the winch – when I notice that the rope has turned over on itself and will lock at the next turn, suspending the bath in mid-air. (The sailors among you will know this is called a riding turn and should be avoided at all costs.)

Realising the winch will not bear the weight of the bath, I manhandle it back into the bathroom, then begin the task of lifting it out through the window on my own.

Eventually the bathroom is clear and I rip back the old vinyl flooring and scrape off the glue to expose ancient wooden floorboards beneath.

Alizée and I scour antique sales and markets to find vintage fittings – a sink and loo – and we've been given a beautiful bateau bath by close friends for a wedding present. This will take its place centre-stage in the newly revamped bathroom.

It is a race against time to get the fittings installed and working, as the nights are closing in. I've taught myself plumbing from YouTube videos, and armed with these new skills, by December we are the proud owners of a functioning new bathroom.

I've reroofed the conservatory and put down a coir matting floor, so it is an ideal place for the dogs to come into the house after a muddy walk. My office adjoins it; they wander in and doze as I work, happy with my proximity.

Alizée has chosen a snug room at the other end of the house for her home study. We are starting to make the place our own.

We are self-sufficient in wood and have brought a log-splitter from France. In the sitting room our wood burner blazes a welcome. And there on the wall is a reminder of Glen Affric, another place we love: a picture of Alizée paddleboarding across the loch with Mabel, a gift from Pippa's mother-in-law, Jane, which she painted herself.

From the windows, sitting on the wooden chair that Dad made more than 40 years ago, I can watch the sheep and see beyond them to our copse and the bluebell wood. Our little house is taking shape.

In such small pleasures contentment lies.

Chapter Fourteen

Pastures New

———

We didn't write a gift list for our wedding – we were just delighted everyone was making the effort to come out to France to celebrate with us – but many kind friends still gave us presents.

Aside from the bath, we were given a dozen Indian Runner ducks – they are distinctive because they stand erect like penguins and run rather than waddle like most ducks. They also honk and squabble and lay beautiful pastel-coloured eggs.

Another friend gave us a dozen fertilised cream Legbar chicken eggs. Legbars lay distinctive pale green and blue eggs and forage for grass, insects, worms, snails and slugs.

I already had an incubator, so I set it up, and by December, ten out of the twelve eggs have hatched into fluffy chicks.

As I didn't have a henhouse, I decided to build one using wood from pallets and an old motorbike trailer, so it became a mobile coop on wheels they could all move into.

Just before we were married, a kind neighbour popped round with another gift. Peter, who has lived in the village for 55 years, brought a tray of vegetables from a garden that everyone envies, as well as some bantam eggs.

Bantams are small, unobtrusive egg-layers. 'Some of the eggs may well be fertilised, so you might get some chicks,' he said. We came back from the wedding, having left our house-sitter in charge of the animals, to find they had hatched.

We called one of the chicks, a cockerel, Peter – in honour of our neighbour – and his girlfriend Lily. They'd sometimes come on picnics with us and eat up all the scraps.

They're here today, scratching for grubs as we watch the changing seasons. When you are new to a house, each day is a revelation: you note how the light falls in different rooms as the sun sets, how green trees turn to burnished copper and gold before the branches of the copses stand bare against the ever-changing sky.

Before long, we are thinking about the sheep we have promised ourselves. Herdwicks, our favourite breed, are from the Lake District. These distinctive little sheep are born with black faces and fleeces so they blend with the rocks of the fells and are less obtrusive to predators when they are young.

As they get older, their fleeces lighten to brown and their faces turn white. Finally they mature into woolly coats of greyish white. Alizée has fallen in love with them too, and by chance a local farmer is looking to move a few on from his own flock, so I agree to take them.

He grins broadly at me when I turn up with my trailer to collect them. His parting words are: 'Good luck to you with them.' I think it is an odd thing to say – but I soon learn why he has cautioned me.

I've filled in their paperwork, checked our hay stocks – there is plenty from the last harvest to take us through the winter – and triple-checked the fencing round the fields to make sure it is secure. Just to be certain, I put the little flock into a small fenced-off area near the house so they can get used to their surroundings.

The next morning, I have a shock. Not a single sheep – except trusty Captain, who has moved with us from Mum and Dad's – remains in the paddock. Apparently they have all jumped the fence. Captain has stayed, I expect, because he is much bigger and less agile and cannot leap out of the enclosure.

I go into a panic and call the dogs, and off we go on a hunt to track down the missing flock. Deploying my best detective skills, I follow the prints of their cloven hooves dinted in the soft soil.

The dogs and I pursue the sheep tracks over a hillside, through a stream and into one of our copses. Then we see tufts of wool snagged on a barbed-wire fence. The sheep have managed to get into a neighbour's field, where they are now happily grazing.

I haven't got a sheepdog, and Ella, though her skills are many and varied, is not a natural herder of sheep. She has absolutely no instinct for it, though I have tried to encourage and train her.

So there is only one thing for it. I must fetch Captain, who during his stay at Mum and Dad's became an honorary sheepdog and learned how to gather and bring in the flock.

Once he is in the field with the errant sheep, all I have to do is shake a bucket full of feed and whistle, and he comes trotting towards me with the Herdwicks hot on his heels. They obey the flock mentality and simply follow each other like . . . sheep.

Then I charge ahead with my bucket of feed, over the fence, through the wood, across the stream and up the hill, until, with Captain leading the flock, all the sheep are back in our field.

When they're safely gathered in, I marvel at their audacity. I couldn't imagine them clearing a metre-high fence, but they seem to think it is great fun to vault it. Every few days they repeat the exercise, and I find them chomping in our neighbour's pasture again.

I start to do a bit of research on this hardy mountain breed. I join the Herdwick Sheep Society and find a common thread. Everyone is remarking that the breed are expert escapologists. The best way to keep them in your field is to put them to graze in the one next door. Then inevitably they'll escape back into the field you want them in and they'll think they've won.

In the Lakes, animals on common land learn over generations where their boundaries are. Ewes teach their lambs. The skill is inbred. It is called hefting, and it is a traditional way of managing animals on large areas of communal grazing.

To establish a heft, sheep have to be kept in place by constant shepherding, because there are no physical boundaries. But once they have learned where their territory is, they stick to it.

Our Herdwicks have now, by and large, learned their boundaries and can roam freely on our acres. But sometimes Alizée and I will be out with the dogs and we'll spot them in a nearby field. One time they followed us to the pub, evidently enjoying the outing, and once again it was Captain who shepherded them home.

All our animals are humanely raised; they have happy, free-range outdoor lives. But as our aim is self-sufficiency, we sell some of our lambs each year to restaurants and local pubs and keep some for our freezer. I'm learning how to butcher them. We have a few broiler chickens, too, that we keep for the pot, and in time we hope to have cattle and goats.

I already have my bees at Bucklebury, but now I introduce a swarm to our farm and build 12 new hives for them, each one containing 50–100,000 bees.

I have been a passionate advocate of bees since I read about Winnie-the-Pooh and his honey jar as a child.

The list of celebrity beekeepers is growing. David Beckham is a devotee. So are actors Leonardo DiCaprio, Morgan Freeman and Scarlett Johansson, as well as rock stars Bruce Springsteen and Peter Balzary (Flea from the Red Hot Chili Peppers). And all have helped to raise the profile of apiculture.

I'd always yearned to keep them, but it wasn't until I turned 24 in 2011 that my wish came true: Mum, Dad and my sisters clubbed together to buy what for me was a wonderful birthday gift.

A delivery van arrived bearing a large buzzing box labelled with the cautionary note: 'Live Bees'. Inside was the nucleus of my colony: 1,000 Buckfast bees. The driver was terrified of picking up the parcel, so I had to collect it from his van.

And so I built up my colony, and now it has multiplied into two: the first at Bucklebury and now one here. Our little farm is growing. We have the bees and sheep, chickens and ducks, our own grazing pastures, a vegetable garden, and a little orchard full of gnarled fruit trees that we want to restore – even a bluebell wood that bursts into pools of indigo blooms in May.

We've unearthed a pond that was so clogged with weeds we didn't even know it was there when we moved in. There is an avenue of oaks and enough fallen wood in our copses to feed the two ravenous wood burners that keep the house snug.

I love the closeness to nature that farming brings. There is something magical about the changing seasons, about going out on a frosty morning, bringing the sheep into the barn for their food and seeing the steam rising from their woolly coats.

Alizée feels fortunate that she only goes up to London twice a week for work – there are good links to Paddington from our local station – and can spend the rest of the time working from her home office.

Although I travel to meetings, I run my business, and the farm of course, from home.

Ella is always at my side. She's a little slower than she was, so she'll jump up and sit beside me on the quad bike while the other dogs run behind as I check the stock. She still sleeps on the floor on my side of the bed; downstairs, she has bagged her cosy spot by the fire-warmed bricks. She is the matriarch of the pack. Because she loves her new home, the others quickly settle too.

It is April 2022, close to my 35th birthday, and Alizée has arranged a treat. We're to go to Thurlestone in Devon to stay with my good friend Nick, his wife, Rosie, and their children.

Nick's family has a holiday home there – I've been visiting it with him since we were 11 – and when Alizée and I arrive, I notice the table has been laid for a dozen or so guests. Suddenly they all jump out from behind sofas and shout, 'Surprise!' I'm delighted that Nick has gathered my closest friends to be with us for this special celebratory weekend.

There is something comforting about the nostalgia of these visits. Sitting here now with such dear friends, their wives and children, I consider both how our lives have changed and how some pleasures remain constant, immutable.

The delight at walking the coastal path is as fresh today as it was 20 years ago. The pleasure of eating an ice cream at Hope Cove is undimmed. Now, though, I stride out with Alizée next to me and a godchild strapped into a harness on my back, while Ella, trotting by my side, shares the final lick of my ice cream cone.

What sticks in my memory are those blissful moments we have with Ella on that trip. We catch the tide at the right moment and swim in the sea together. She loves our coastal walks. She scampers beside me along the beach, stands on a boogie board and surfs the waves with me, digs holes in the sand and lies in them. Then, at the end of a long day, her coat fluffy with salt spray, she falls into a contented sleep.

Back home, Ella's happy times stay with me. Then May rolls around and Laurence has decided to sell Le Moulin: it is time to pack up her memories and move on. She'll go to Bormes-les-Mimosas, which will become her permanent home.

There are lots of treasures that Jean Gabriel amassed at Le Moulin, and Alizée is keen to bring some of them back to the farm, so we hitch our six-metre trailer to the car and drive to the Channel Tunnel, then on to Limoges to load them up.

There are ancient beams that Jean Gabriel saved when he restored the mill and which we intend to make into a bench – with a plaque in memory of him – to put in a tranquil spot.

There is the shell of an old Romany caravan that we want to restore, an antique donkey cart, a dilapidated old tractor; all of them will be loaded onto the trailer and transported to the farm.

We pack the trailer carefully, dismantling and reassembling, using the space as efficiently as possible. Even so, our load looks huge and cumbersome. I think about the height restrictions on the tunnels we have to drive through, and realise with rising panic that our three-and-a-half-metre-high load won't go through them.

So Alizée looks at the map and we choose an alternative route, manoeuvring our giant load of ill-sorted memorabilia through circuitous byways that avoid all low bridges and tunnels – until we find ourselves unexpectedly outside the Palace of Versailles.

Not quite knowing how we've got here, I plough on, trusting Alizée's navigation skills as the streets get narrower and narrower and we squeeze past parked cars and edge onto kerbs in an effort to avoid oncoming vehicles.

We need to be at Calais in time for our train and we have just two hours to spare. I think back to the day of the cupcake delivery and hope the journey won't be similarly calamitous.

Finally we end up back on the motorway and arrive just in time, but customs are vigilant and seem perturbed by our unwieldy load. They inspect it minutely, even turning out everything we've packed neatly into the caravan to make sure no stowaway is hiding inside.

They look hard at the strange amalgam of goods. They suck in their cheeks and tut.

Then Alizée, wearing her best conciliatory smile, explains in French that these are precious memorabilia from her family home, and finally they are appeased and wave us through.

It is the early hours when we get back to the farm. We're delighted to have brought a little bit of Alizée's French heritage back with us to Berkshire. I may have abandoned a Renault van in northern France, but we've acquired in its place a donkey cart, an old tractor and an antique Romany caravan. It seems like a fair exchange.

That summer we're invited by friends to join them on a trip to Alaska. It is the opportunity of a lifetime. We think of it as our honeymoon; a chance to swim among glaciers, to watch wildlife, to fish for salmon. Our only regret is that Ella is not with us.

It is hard to take in the wonder of it all. We know, although we have not yet seen them, that bears and wolves stalk the icy wastes. In the glacial waters we spot sea lions, humpback whales, schools of dolphins and porpoises. There are frozen rivers and mountains iced with snow – and we see them all at close quarters, with friends, from a beautiful pre-war wood-hulled boat.

One morning I wake early and stand on the deck watching the new morning unfold, scanning the shoreline to see if I can glimpse a black bear or a grizzly. My host joins me while the others sleep on, and we decide to go on a recce, a little early-morning adventure.

We intend to go salmon fishing later in the day, so we jump into a smaller boat and motor up the creek to look for places to fish. The river meanders and we find our way blocked by a fallen tree. We run aground and the boat's propeller gets clogged with stones.

Armed with my practical skills, I set to work clearing the debris with a Swiss army knife I always keep in my pocket. Meanwhile my friend goes ashore to explore.

I'm waist-deep in water with my head down by the propeller when suddenly I hear a cry from the beach. It's my friend. 'Hey, bear!' he shouts.

I look up, startled.

'Come and look at this,' he calls.

I abandon my task, tether the boat and run ashore. What I see startles me. There in the sand are the unmistakable paw prints of a wolf . . . and a little further on, fresh bear droppings.

I feel a shudder, both thrilled and fearful that we are surrounded by predators. My heart is pumping wildly. My friend and I run back to the boat and I set to clearing the propeller with new vigour. We need to move quickly. We don't want to encounter the bear.

The little boat's engine throbs back into life and we chug back to find our friends sitting down to breakfast. We have huge, relieved grins on our faces.

'What have you two been up to?' one of the group asks. We smile knowingly at each other but do not share our experience. And when we all go salmon fishing later that day, we make sure we're well armed with plenty of bear-repellent spray.

Chapter Fifteen

A Sadness Too Deep for Words

———

Back home, thoughts return to our pack; I'm thinking about breeding from Mabel.

The search is on for a mate for her, a suitable golden retriever dog – and I find him on the front cover of *Country Life*. A superstar!

Providence has a hand in it, too: I notice in the credits that the photographer is Millie Pilkington, who has taken many photos of our family over the years.

So it seems somehow fitting that this handsome dog should be a match for Mabel. I go to visit his owner to check his lineage. I find out all I can about him: how are his eyes, his hips – these are the challenges faced by retrievers – and Alizée jokes that humans are far less scrupulous about who they have kids with.

I get acquainted with his owner over a cuppa while he and Mabel have an amiable sniff around each other. Ella comes with us, of course. If she is wary, I would be, but she seems to enjoy the canine company and the deal is made. Once Mabel is in season we'll return.

The day arrives and we're off to Wiltshire again. The mating game isn't as easy as you'd think. Mabel is a novice and we have to get her locked on to the dog by holding them both in place. It's called 'the tie', and to be sure it's worked we must be certain Mabel doesn't wriggle away for 20 minutes or so.

So I'm standing face to face with her mate's owner making small talk while we hold our dogs in position and the ritual takes place. After five minutes we've covered all the pleasantries. After ten I've opened every conversational gambit I can think of, and we're standing in uncomfortably close proximity, looking into each other's eyes in embarrassed silence.

I'm relieved when it's over, Mabel (and I) can have a rest and then we're off home. And within five weeks comes the happy news that she's pregnant.

Meanwhile the Duke of Richmond has invited me to open the first ever Goodwoof event at Goodwood House in Sussex. It's a glorious festival of all things canine, and Ella and I will be in the forefront of an opening parade of 240 spaniels.

The dukes of Richmond have always been famously fond of their dogs. The Kennels, where this dog extravaganza is held, was designed in 1787 as a stately home for their pets by celebrated Georgian architect James Wyatt.

Even then, it seems, dogs had a special place in the nation's hearts: The Kennels had its central heating system installed 100 years before Goodwood House itself.

Zulu, Inka and Nala also join the Goodwoof opening parade, but it is Ella who revels most in the attention, sitting in the dog carriage behind my bike, graciously greeting all comers. Every time I see a beaming face coming towards me, I smile welcomingly – only to discover that it's Ella they've come to meet, not me, and she can't wait to say hello.

During this wonderful summer of 2022 we experience a heatwave, and we have a second harvest. I drive my old tractor across the fields, skimming off the extra cutting of grass, and the dogs sit in the shade of the trees and watch me turn the hay.

Mabel's pregnancy is nearing its end and the heat is challenging for her. She and Ella find the coolest place in the farm – the stone floor of the cold store under the house, just bricks on soil – and lie flat on their bellies letting the welcome chill seep through their bodies.

I take the dogs for pre-dawn and late-evening walks to avoid the searing heat.

Mabel's pups arrive, bang on their due date, on the hottest July day for centuries. There are eight of them: four boys, four girls. All healthy. All but one of the pups is accounted for, and this is when I say to Alizée, trying to keep the wheedling tone out of my voice: 'We are keeping one, aren't we?'

'Do we really need another dog?' she asks.

Of course we don't. But we keep one anyway. Isla joins the family, and the next eight weeks, as a glorious summer slips into golden autumn and the pups are weaned and gaining in confidence and independence, are blissful.

I'm reminded of Monty Don, who a couple of years earlier lost his beloved golden retriever Nigel. Gentle and affectionate, Nigel became Monty's inadvertent co-star on the BBC's *Gardeners' World*: there was never a plan to make him a canine star, but he just loved the camera and, biding his time patiently through the endless hours of filming, seemed to know intuitively where and how to strike the best pose.

I got to know Monty not through his gardening so much as his dogs. It all started when one of his sons saw me cycling in London, the dogs in their cart in front of my bike, and took a photo of us.

'Doesn't that dog look just like Nellie?' he asked his dad, thinking one of Monty's other dogs bore a distinct resemblance to Mabel.

Monty agreed that the likeness was striking, and when I ring to ask him if he'd like one of Mabel's pups, he's delighted. He chooses a puppy he names Ned, now much beloved by his family as well as viewers of *Gardeners' World*.

What stays with me from our meeting is Alizée's horror that I did not give her warning that such an illustrious horticulturalist would be visiting. She was embarrassed by the state of our flower borders, savaged by eight puppies.

I am donating one of Mabel's pups to Guide Dogs for the Blind, too. During the pandemic, the dogs' breeding programme was paused and there is now a desperate shortage of new pups coming through for training.

Occasionally the programme welcomes new dogs and, subject to health checks, it is settled: one of Mabel's pups will be trained for a working career as a guide dog. I agree to raise the funds for this, and for his eventual retirement.

In return, I am allowed to name my potential guide dog. As I have fond memories of the Queen, I call him Bertie, after her father.

I've always been awestruck by the abilities and aptitudes, the loyalty and reliability of service dogs. I don't believe we have yet tapped into their full potential. The scope and scale of their capacities is vast. They track ivory poachers, detect illicit drugs, sniff out explosives.

Medical detection dogs identify diseases like cancer in its early stages from urine samples; others trace leprosy from residual scent on a garment. Their olfactory powers are so fine-tuned that the owner of the clothing can be miles – even continents – away.

Then there are the resourceful, hard-working dogs that assist mountain search-and-rescue teams; and the water-loving Newfoundlands who have a strong instinct for saving lives at sea.

Brave police and military dogs deserve our unstinting admiration, too.

So when the Dogs' Trust invite me to present an award to a top police dog and his handler, I readily agree.

It was early September 2022 when, togged up in black tie, I went off with Ella to the formal awards ceremony in London. But I'd barely arrived when my phone buzzed. A message from Mum. The Queen, she told me, had just passed away.

Such news percolates swiftly, and I heard hushed whispers spread round the room. I could not stay. Politely I made my quiet apologies, congratulating both police dog and handler, then drove home, memories crowding in on me, thoughts of our great monarch and her years of unstinting service to the nation.

I remembered learning about her in school, and as I watched her funeral, with Ella on my lap, I was overawed by the spectacle. But what caught me off guard and made me cry was the moment when the procession passed her pony and her adored corgis. The Queen's animals, this sense that they too had lost someone so dear to them, was what prompted my tears.

The sombre mood persisted beyond the nation's mourning. My beloved Ella was visibly ageing. When Mabel's pups were 12 weeks old and due for their second vaccination, she came with me to the vet's. She liked to go with me – there was no fear or trepidation – and I mentioned to Mark in passing that her coat had lost a bit of its lustre. Perhaps it was the hot weather, but she was eating less, too.

Mark took some bloods, just to check that all was well, and we went home.

Then came the phone call.

Within an instant of hearing Mark's voice – his tentative 'Hi, James' – I knew. There was bad news. I remember closing my eyes. 'Have you got the blood test results?'

'It's not good,' he said. Ella had kidney failure. Her kidneys were barely functioning at all. Mark, who had cared for her since her first vaccination, was now telling me she had two weeks to live.

I couldn't speak. Everything stopped. Tears choked me. I remember an awful, deadening numbness. I couldn't frame the questions that crowded into my mind. Eventually I broke the silence. 'Can I call you back?'

It was hours before I trusted myself to speak, to phone the vet. 'What can I do to make her last days as comfortable as possible?' I asked.

There was Ella beside me. She still wagged her tail. She still wanted to come out with me. She seemed just a little slower and older. But ever faithful, ever sure, and not showing signs of such a dire prognosis.

Mark prescribed fluid therapy to flush out the toxins in her system. She'd feel better afterwards, he assured me. And he recommended a bland diet; none of the rich treats – like cheese titbits and pâté – that she loved.

So we went back to the vet's and Ella was put on a saline drip. They'd observe her for 48 hours, Mark told me.

I wanted to stay there with her, but I steeled myself to leave her, assuring her gently that I'd be back soon.

The next morning, at 8 a.m., I went to visit her. I lay on the floor, my head next to hers in her pen. She had tubes going into her, but when she saw me, she lifted her head and her tail thumped her bed.

I had a pocketful of food – a mix of treats to tempt her and the bland food she was supposed to eat – and I fed her little cubes of cheddar and the freeze-dried carrots she loved.

I chatted to her, as I always did, telling her she must eat and that it would be okay. 'You can't go yet. I need you to stick around for a bit longer,' I said, and as the salty tears ran down my face, she licked them away.

I lay there next to her for more than an hour. I didn't want to go, but I knew she needed to rest. Driving home without her, I felt the dull ache of grief. There was also guilt at leaving her – I knew she'd be happier at home – and I imagined the stressful yearning she'd feel on her own.

I tried to process in my mind the awful conflict of it: she had seemed quite healthy, just a bit off-colour. But the fact was she was going to die soon. It was the beginning of the end of my time with Ella, my companion through my darkest hours, my most trusted friend; the dog who saved my life.

I could not bear to tell anyone because it made it more real. Alizée was the only person who knew.

While Ella was at the vet's – during those interminable 48 hours – I clung on to the hope of a miracle. Perhaps they could do something. Maybe her poorly functioning kidneys would hold out if we managed her diet.

But after two days, they said there was nothing more they could do. At 14, Ella was simply too old. A dog will die of something, and her fate was to die of kidney failure.

So the hope ebbed away, and when I went to collect her I knew she was coming home to see out her final days.

In the meantime, I wanted to squeeze every drop of joy out of my life with her. I didn't want to leave her side for a second.

I still couldn't frame the words to tell my family that she was dying. Alizée offered to do it, but eventually I said I'd call Mum.

'Hi, darling,' she said.

The words froze on my lips. I couldn't say anything.

'Hello, are you there?' said Mum, bewildered by my silence.

Alizée took the phone from me to break the news, and I walked away, tears coursing down my face. It was the hardest part, this public acknowledgement that Ella was dying, that any time she had left on earth was a bonus.

I try to be normal with her, to act as if nothing untoward has happened, to enjoy our waning hours together, but it is almost impossible when my sadness manifests as a physical pain.

Dogs are sensitive to changes in mood; they intuit every tiny gradation of thought and feeling, and Ella's instinct is still sharp. So I steel myself to be strong for her sake.

We walk to the sweet chestnut tree in the middle of the field, a place where we love to be. We drive to see Mike, his wife Sophie and their spaniel, Ella's brother Otto. Ella still loves the car, and she enjoys the journey.

Once at Mike and Sophie's house in Wiltshire, Ella trots off to find Otto.

'She looks fine,' says Mike, enveloping me in a hug.

'But she's not,' I counter, my eyes welling.

We've discussed, many times, the ache of loss we'd feel without our dogs. But now it is almost here, and I cannot articulate the sheer depth of my sadness.

When we have lunch, Ella sits at my feet under the table, her head in my lap, as she always does at mealtimes. She has not eaten anything yet today, and when a piece of pâté falls from my plate she gulps it down.

'So pâté it is,' I say to myself.

It is too rich for her failing kidneys, but it is better than starving, so that is what she shall have.

After lunch we go for a little wander, the four of us – Mike and me, Alizée and Sophie – with Ella and Otto, and afterwards we take a photo of the dogs. Siblings together for the last time. It is a cherished moment.

Back at home, I think about the vet's prognosis. Two weeks have passed; three have merged into four. Ella is trooping on. Then the

JAMES MIDDLETON

weeks become months and she defies every expectation. So I decide to take her on a sentimental journey, to all the places she loves best.

We go to the Lakes, to the cottage where we have stayed so many times. She cannot do our usual fell walk, so we shorten it. She does not sprint ahead as she used to do, but walks with slow and measured steps, turning her head to look back at me, as she always did.

She sleeps a lot. She is dying, but she is happy.

On every trip, at every turn, we are together. She comes to church, as she always has, and sits at my feet. And whenever I pull on my boots, she is ready to walk alongside me.

Ella has always been the only one of my dogs to sleep in my bedroom, and she still sleeps there now with Alizée and me. She alone is allowed to sit beside me on the sofa, and as the nights draw in and the fire is lit, she snuggles beside me while I leaf through the photo albums that chart her life.

I reminisce in the firelight, Ella lying on her favourite Herdwick sheepskin we bought in the Lakes, in a shop near Windermere. Our own flock of them now graze our Berkshire fields.

There are days when I smile and feel grateful to Ella for hanging on so I have time to adjust to the fact that she is going. 'Thank you for letting me process this,' I tell her. She is, I'm sure, planning her exit to make it manageable for me.

On our travels, we go back to the South Kensington Club, where Ella introduced me to Alizée. We amble down Old Church Street, past our flat and into the church garden where we used to walk four times a day for over ten years.

Weekends are tailored to suit her needs and capabilities. We go for short walks then loop back to the house so she can have a nap.

During this time, as Ella's life is gently ebbing away, our excitable pup Isla is beginning her life's adventure, and the two dogs form an unlikely bond. Isla, it seems, makes Ella young again; Ella even initiates the games they play together.

And as I watch them play – my dying old dog, our new pup – my eyes blur with tears.

It is a warm, soft afternoon in September and we're at Goodwood again. Ella is walking her favourite tracks, smelling the familiar scents, and she seems to be fired by fresh energy. She is perkier than usual; it is lovely to watch her sniff the air and scamper off.

Then, as we near the car, her back legs give way and she collapses sideways. I rush to her, panicked, my first thought: 'She's dying, she's had a heart attack.' But when I get to her, she is still breathing, her eyes are open, and tentatively she lifts her head.

I scoop her up, take her to the car, gently coax her to drink some water. I sit with her, stricken. Twenty minutes later, she tries to stand, but I tell her soothingly to stay.

So the moment passes and I conclude that Ella, lost in the moment, forgot her capabilities, simply enjoyed herself a bit too much that day. But the slow deterioration continues.

By mid-October she is noticeably weaker, her capacities waning. She does not walk as far, and when the weather starts to turn – the nights are chilly and the morning air freighted with frost – I fall asleep beside her in the lamplight by the flickering fire.

And that is when the idea comes to me to document her life, to honour her in a book and, in a way, through it to immortalise her. Without Ella I would not be here. I would not be with Alizée.

Ella is responsible for making me happier than I could ever have imagined.

My thoughts wander further. Ella will never meet any future children we may have, and that makes me sad.

But still she soldiers on, and December arrives with the promise of Christmas. She goes with us again to Chelsea Old Church for the carol service, sitting under the pew, warming my feet as she always does, listening to the familiar tunes.

There is solace and safety for me in the rituals of religion: the peace of the church seeps into me; the quiet is restorative. In the past, I've gone to this church – All Saints, by our flat – just to process my thoughts. I do not have to have a reason to be there; that is the wonder of it.

But today Ella and I enjoy the carols. Or at least I do. I belt them out tunelessly, and I'm sure she is embarrassed.

Then we're off to see the Christmas lights, and Alizée and I discuss what we'll do over the festive season, knowing Ella will come first.

Alizée's family are going skiing in the French Alps, and coincidentally, my family is also planning a New Year holiday there.

Is it safe for Ella to travel with us? We consult the vet and he gives his approval. He'll just flush out the toxins from her system first to perk her up.

And so we pack up the car to drive to France. Ella always loves car journeys, and once she realises we're packing, she makes sure to get in the way. She doesn't want to miss out.

We give her the priority seat, Mabel alongside her. Isla and our other dogs stay at home with our house-sitter and we set off early to catch Le Shuttle across the Channel.

Late that same day, we arrive in the Alps. The air has a glacial freshness; there is the deep, peaceful silence that follows snowfall. And all around the valley the chalet lights twinkle.

Ella rushes out to roll in the snow – she loves the icy thrill of it – then ambles into the chalet to say hi to my parents. It's been a long journey, but she isn't remotely troubled by the trip.

The next day, while the rest of the family get their ski passes, Alizée and I go ski touring with Mabel, hiking through the snowfields and skiing down slopes. Ella stays in the chalet – someone is always with her – so we make it a short trip and return to her tail-wagging welcome.

She enjoys her holiday and sleeps well; her responses seem quicker, her mind more alert. We wonder if the altitude actually helps – she clearly loves being in the mountains – although we know the air is thinner and we're conscious her body must work harder.

This is our last Christmas with Ella and it is a wonderful one – the company and the change of pace and scene have all given her a spring in her step. When we get home, she is glad to be reunited with the other dogs and we settle back into a routine.

But just as I start to count my blessings – Ella has, after all, defied the vet's prognosis and lived for a further three months – she begins to deteriorate. And this time the downturn happens swiftly.

I carry her upstairs to bed now, and often I wake worrying that she is no longer breathing, so I put my hand on her to feel the gentle rise and fall, to make sure. I sense her slow breaths getting weaker by the day.

I do not want her to suffer, so I call the vet and ask him, 'When is the right time to put her to sleep?' because I know she is slowly going.

'When she can no longer eat and is visibly uncomfortable, that is the time,' Mark tells me. 'I am on standby for you,' he reassures me.

We agree that she must not feel pain; her life must not be prolonged beyond that point. I know her death is imminent.

I am with her now for every second of the day. She can still walk – slowly, tentatively; just a short distance – so I carry her outside and watch as she wanders round and sniffs at her favourite places.

My eye is ever alert for the subtlest change in her well-being. Each day she still sits in her bed at my feet as I work.

Then one day, as I carry her downstairs in the morning, she loses control of her bladder and pees on me. It doesn't matter to me, but it is a sign that her time is near.

I clean her up, settle her on her bed and Isla cuddles next to her; I have this wonderful photo of them together, one of the last. Then I call the vet and say, 'It's near the end.'

We make a plan. He says he's willing to come to our house to sleep over himself the following night. And so the day progresses.

Ella has always had a wonderful look in her eyes, a look of devotion. And even now, it is still here. She seems to look into my soul. She knows me better than any human, and I capture this unflinching loyalty in a last photo of her. It is still my screen saver today.

As the waning day inches into dusk, I lie on the sofa next to her. I know it will be our last night together and I do not want to go to sleep. I sit her in my lap and say to her: 'Thank you for being everything I could ever have asked of you and more.

'It is okay to go now. You do not need to fight any more.'

She has given me everything, and those words are a release. Her breathing gets slower and weaker. She is not suffering, but her breaths become shallower, more laboured. I know she has hours left to live.

My beloved Ella is fading.

Chapter Sixteen

A Final Farewell . . . and New Beginnings

––––

It is 3 a.m. on 7 January 2023 when Ella takes her last breath. I feel the inhalation and wait, wait, but there is no breath out.

Her eyes are closed and I touch her eyelids. Not a flicker or twitch of nerve. I remember sobbing. I say my goodbyes. Again I say, 'Thank you for saving my life, for everything you've done to make my life easier, better. Actually complete. Thank you for being with me through everything.'

I make sure I tell her I will be fine. I'll manage because she has taught me how to. She's set me up with everything, with Alizée. I'll be okay.

Then I stroke her and tell her it is time for her to go and find Tilly and Mini in the Elysian Fields.

Alizée stayed up most of the night with me, but just before the end she went upstairs to bed. So I had my time alone with Ella. I continue to lie there with her, and it is strange to see the shift in her once she has gone.

Even a sleeping dog shows signs of life, but something has left Ella's body. It's comforting in a way. Her struggle has ended. There has been no gasping for breath. She literally slipped away. A peaceful death.

I do not want to move from her side. An hour passes and, exhausted, I close my eyes. My hands are still on her as I fall asleep, her body on my lap. And so the early hours pass into a grey dawn.

At about 6.30 a.m., Alizée came downstairs and I jolted awake, saw Ella again – inert, cold now – and burst into tears.

Alizée knew immediately that Ella had passed, and we had a moment together, all three of us. Ella was now stiff and cold and it was hard to witness this change in her, the shift from life to death.

She had brought us together, Alizée and me, and it was because of her that we were married and living under this roof, in our own house. And now, for the first time in our lives as a couple, we would be without her.

I knew there were quiet rituals I needed to observe. I had to get up, find Ella's bed and put her to rest lying comfortably in it, swaddled in her favourite Herdwick rug.

I brushed her for the last time, laid her gently in her bed and covered her body with the sheepskin. She looked peaceful.

I remember again feeling grateful that she had not died abruptly, that we'd had those last golden months together to say goodbye. And I had already made plans for her burial.

I wanted her to lie next to our other dogs in my parents' garden, and in the daytime after she had died – on the Saturday – I started to dig, the tears streaming down my face.

There is a conundrum at the heart of this. I did not want to bury Ella in the cold earth. I didn't want to say the grave was finished. So I dug and dug – the exhaustion, the physical exertion was a kind of catharsis – because I could not bear to say my last goodbye.

We had agreed, the family and I, that they should all come to the burial on Sunday. That was when everyone could gather – my sisters, their husbands and children – to say their last farewell to Ella.

So we kept her cool, and that morning I took her in my arms for one last walk round the garden. We had spent such a huge amount of her life there at Bucklebury, it was fitting that this should be her final journey and resting place.

I had lined the grave with hay I'd taken from my fields late that summer – Ella had sat by me on the tractor as I'd harvested it – and all the family stood round as I lowered her into the pit I had dug.

She was wrapped in her sheepskin, and I tucked her in tenderly, put some hay on top of her. Then I asked the children to put their own handful of hay on her and each of them said a little prayer. Ella had touched all their lives.

Everyone was crying by now. Ella had stolen all our hearts.

And then everyone, bar me, went inside. I wanted to be alone to finish burying her, to have my final glimpse of her before she was fully covered, before I said my last goodbye.

I read 'What I Learned about Love, I Learned from my Dog' to her, the same poem that had been read at our wedding. There are lines in it that still spring to my lips:

When someone is having a bad day, be silent, sit close by and
    nuzzle them gently . . .
Delight in the simple joy of a long walk together.
Love each other unconditionally.

And then the hardest part, letting her go. I remember taking a
deep breath and shovelling on the soil. I channelled all the positive
thoughts I had about our time together and I finished the grave
with gusto.

I had made a little wooden cross – the same as Tilly's and
Mini's – and I placed it at the top of the grave, a temporary measure
before I got her headstone.

Then I sat alone with my thoughts, salt tears running down my
face; no Ella to lick them away now.

I do not know how long I sat there crying – it could have been
minutes or hours – before my father came out with a little glass
of whisky for me. He made a toast to Ella and we drank together.

Dad went back into the house, but I stayed outside as the
darkness gathered. I did not want to leave Ella alone. I did not want
to go inside.

So I lit candles and lanterns and sat with her until the pitch-black
enveloped me. I did not want her to spend her first night in the cold
earth alone.

I tried so hard to think of the positives; the happiness that Ella
had brought to so many, all that she had given me, but the sadness
was a suffocating shroud.

The family came out intermittently to give me another little tot of
whisky, and when I eventually went back into the house, the children

were all tucked up in bed. Everyone hugged me and we opened a bottle of champagne to toast Ella and celebrate her life.

The meal we ate – belatedly – on the night of 9 January could not have been lovelier because everyone reminisced about Ella. There was laughter among the chatter, funny stories among the sad.

We talked well into the early hours about all our beloved dogs: Pippa and James's Raffa, Catherine and William's Lupo and Orla, then Zulu, Inka, Luna and Nala – all of them Ella's offspring.

I have a treasured miniature portrait of Ella in a tiny embossed frame. It was painted by a friend, the artist Holly Frean, who sent it to me not long after we lost Ella, with a kind note of condolence.

I carry it with me every time I go on an adventure I think Ella would have enjoyed, or to a big event where, before Alizée came into my life, she would have been my plus-one. (If I'm just going to the shops, I'll probably leave it at home.)

The portrait has a twofold purpose: I like to think of Ella still sharing the highlights of my life, and it also gives me confidence to know she is there when my nerves need calming. I just reach for her in my pocket and feel reassured. I have it with me now.

The week that followed passed in a blur of grief. For 15 years Ella had been beside me; her absence was like a physical ache. Tears would come unbidden to my eyes. I barely held it together. Then, one ice-bound day when the hedgerows were rimed stiff with frost, I went out to collect some logs at the farm.

It was mid-afternoon and I was throwing them into the wheelbarrow and then loading them onto the trailer to bring back to the house when Alizée came rushing out, her hair dripping wet after a shower, wearing just a skirt, a T-shirt and wellies.

She was mouthing something at me, desperate to make herself heard above the chug of the tractor engine.

I thought something must be wrong. She wasn't dressed for going out on such a cold day. Then I saw there were tears in her eyes.

'I'm pregnant!' she yelled as I cut the engine.

'Are you sure?' I asked, and when she nodded and said she was certain, we both gave a huge whoop of joy and hugged each other so hard we could barely catch our breath. I felt a wonderful, exhilarating rush of happiness. Our own little miracle.

My next thought was: 'We must get you back to the house, in the warm.' So we ran inside, I lit the fire and we sat together bound up in the thrill of it, this new life to come.

'It's such a shame Ella didn't know about it,' I said.

'But she did,' insisted Alizée. She was certain that in those early weeks of her pregnancy, when unknown even to us our baby had begun to form inside her, Ella would have detected those subtle hormonal shifts that signal new life.

She used to sit with her head resting against Alizée's tummy. 'I've been pregnant for a month or so. Ella would have known before we did,' she said.

She was adamant. If dogs can sense a drop in blood sugar, if they can detect cancer, surely Ella – the most intuitive of dogs – would have recognised the change in her, she reasoned.

And I agreed. She must be right. The thought made me smile. I remembered now, too, that Ella had spent much more time with

Alizée in the weeks before her death. She would come in from a walk with me and immediately go for a cuddle with her.

It all figured now. It made sense. Ella knew. And she chose her timing impeccably. We had our weeks to mourn her – and then she slipped away just before the excitement of Alizée's pregnancy.

There was a fitting symmetry to it: Ella had relinquished her hold on life to make way for our new baby. Her job was done. She had set me on the right path and now it was time for her to bow out. A sad end heralded a bright new beginning.

The thought comforted and sustained me.

Alizée's pregnancy is not without problems. She catches COVID almost as soon as she knows she is pregnant, then gets bouts of bad morning sickness. Fortunately it is not like Catherine's sickness – it abates after the first few months – but she seems constantly to be rushing between the bathroom and Zoom meetings for work.

I take on cooking duties, and once she is feeling better, Alizée starts craving potatoes. I rack my brains to think of different ways of serving them up. Dauphinoise, tartiflette, sautéed . . .

Of course my little portrait of Ella comes with me when I go with Alizée for her scans and check-ups.

We come home proudly with our first blurred image of our baby and stick it on the fridge next to the scans of the pups Ella had over the years.

I want Alizée to feel confident and supported – besides, I'm excited to go myself – and I do not miss one hospital visit. Alizée teases me, as I always have hundreds of questions for the midwives and sonographers.

'James thinks he's an expert because he's had a few litters of puppies,' she jokes, telling me, 'I'm surprised you're not getting Mabel's whelping box out for me.'

The months pass, and during the wet summer of 2023 there is no respite from the rain to get the hay in. Alizée's due date is looming and I'm panicking that I won't get the grass cut and turned in time to store it away for the winter.

Then September brings a mini heatwave, and when I spot that a few fine days are forecast, I get up before dawn to start cutting the grass in the meadow.

I chug along on the tractor for a few hours, making the most of the dry day, then decide it's time to stop for breakfast. I've barely got through the back door when Alizée rushes in to remind me: 'James, it's my last scan today. We'll have to leave for the hospital in five minutes.'

I dash upstairs to shower, pull on clean jeans and a shirt – I don't even have time to find a pair of boxer shorts – and Alizée thrusts a Thermos mug of tea at me as we rush out to the car to drive to Basingstoke hospital.

We've called upon our wonderful NHS to take care of Alizée. Mum had all three of us in NHS hospitals, and we know the first-class care we've already had will continue through to our baby's birth.

We arrive at the hospital expecting a brief visit and check-up. Alizée still has a week or so to go and this is just a final reassurance before the birth. Scans normally take 20 minutes or so, and I decide to leave my flask of tea in the car to drink afterwards.

We make our way to the ultrasound room. The normally chatty team seem a bit subdued today as they run the probe over Alizée's tummy.

'You're going to have a baby . . .' begins the sonographer.

'Yes, we know that,' we chorus, smiling.

'. . . today,' he continues. 'Your baby is ready to come out, so we really need to get you wired up to a monitor now.'

It emerges that the levels of amniotic fluid – which protect the foetus from trauma – are precariously low and our baby needs to be delivered quickly.

We gulp. This is a complete surprise. Alizée hasn't yet begun her maternity leave from work; she hasn't brought her grab bag. I'm not even wearing underpants. 'Can we pop home and get our stuff?' we plead.

'No, we really need to get you in now,' comes the reply.

So within half an hour Alizée is being wired up and induced. Luckily, her mum and grandparents, who are going to help after the baby is born, are already at our house, so I call Laurence and fill her in on the unexpected news.

Next, I make a call to my own mum: her seventh grandchild is on its way! Later that day, she and Laurence appear at the hospital with all the bits and pieces Alizée needs, as well as our baby's car seat (and my underpants).

I smile to myself: I remembered to bring Ella's portrait but didn't have time to put on boxer shorts.

Alizée's contractions begin. But evening segues into night and the baby does not arrive. I settle down to sleep on the floor by her bed, but she struggles to get any rest as her contractions get stronger.

Next morning I make toast and tea in the patients' kitchen. The smells remind me of boarding school; familiar, evocative. We eat together and sip our tea thinking, 'Today we'll become parents.'

We've started to think about names – they have to work in both French and English – and we've sketched out a list. But our baby is still slow to arrive.

Neither of us wants to be cooped up in the hospital all day, so, with permission, we go for a walk in a nearby park, relishing the fresh air, the autumnal beauty of it all. We make 35 laps in all and hope the exercise will encourage the baby to move.

Alizée's contractions get stronger and closer together, but still no baby. I spend another night on the hospital floor and Alizée sleeps even more fitfully.

Then at midday on 20 September she goes into labour. Mum planned to bring the dogs so we could all go for another walk in the park – but now Alizée is wondering if Mabel could come in and be her support dog while she gives birth. After all, Mabel had her own litter of pups only last year. But I conclude that it would be a tall order for PAT to register her to come into the maternity ward in time. So Alizée will have to settle for me as her birth partner.

Although I've delivered dozens of puppies and lambs, I find myself confounded. I wish I could help Alizée take away her pain and bear it myself, and the fact that I can't frustrates me.

I've brought a playlist – the songs we played on our first long car journey to the Lake District together – and I hope it will sustain, soothe and energise her.

Time seems to melt away, minutes graduate seamlessly into hours and I cannot keep track of their passing. Outside a storm brews and I watch a beech tree by the window shudder and sway. But there is no noise inside – we're protected from the howling of the wind – and the lights are now dim in the room as I watch Alizée. I cannot believe her strength.

I thought I loved her as much as I possibly could, but now the beauty and wonder of childbirth is teaching me even more about her resilience and power.

I do not realise it, but the hours have ticked by and midnight has passed into the early morning of 21 September when our beautiful baby boy arrives. I am beyond emotional; too caught up in the wonder and glory of it all even for tears.

I find myself with a pair of scissors, cutting the umbilical cord, and then Alizée is cradling our son and my arms are encircling both of them. Then Alizée, who has had two days without rest, falls into a deep sleep while I undo my shirt and our baby lies on my chest, skin to skin, and I sit and look at him in silent awe.

I am transfixed by the perfection of him: his miniature hands and nails, his tiny feet; his little scrunched nose and ears. I listen to his breaths, the first few breaths of this new life, and watch the rise and fall of his chest.

I am exhausted, but too full of the miracle of birth to think about sleep, so quietly, with a sense that I must not break the delicate magic of the spell, I just watch our new baby son.

And then I get out my little portrait of Ella. I have tears in my eyes as I think back to the day Alizée first told me she was pregnant and our boy's life, barely the size of a golf ball, was just beginning in her belly.

Now, nine months on, he is here with us, and I am introducing him to Ella.

Three hours pass. Nurses and medics come and go, barely noticed as I lie with our baby, savouring those first precious hours of his life in the half-light of the new day.

I gaze at him, the image etched into my heart. Nothing can prepare you for parenthood, no matter how much they tell you about the marvel of it all. I had not imagined the scope, the power and the glory of it.

And in those early hours of his life, as I promise to protect and care for him, I also know I will tell him all about Ella. The stories are already here in my head, ready to spill out.

I look across at Alizée. She is waking up again and our baby goes straight into her arms. We are laughing now. 'Can you believe he is really ours; that he's actually here?' we say.

Alizée is starving hungry, so off I go to make more toast. I have a new dad's proud grin on my face as I pop the bread into the toaster and switch on the kettle. I watch as dads-to-be walk into the maternity unit with pregnant soon-to-be mums. I hear, too, the wail of a newborn.

Another new dad is warming milk. We are all part of the same tribe now. Parents. We cannot hide our joy.

When I come back to Alizée with her tea and toast, our baby has latched on and is breastfeeding for the first time. Morning has arrived and we're now in a postnatal room, just the three of us. Or actually four if you count Ella (which I do.)

I touch her little picture in its gilt frame in my pocket. Then I change our son's nappy – the second one I've done since his birth – handling him like precious porcelain, desperate not to hurt him with my fat sausage fingers as I do the poppers up on his weeny sleepsuit and place him carefully back into his mum's arms.

Then there is his name. We have thought about it – of course we have – and we decide on it now. Inigo Gabriel Middleton. Inigo means fiery, ardent, although he is peaceful now. Gabriel is in memory of his grandfather, Alizée's papa. It is a small tribute and we look forward to sharing lots of stories about his French grandad too.

Almost from the moment Inigo was born, Alizée has been asking me: 'Do you think we can go home now?' I go to speak to the matron. 'It's up to you,' she says, 'but I was thinking about tomorrow.'

'Alizée is feeling good. Inigo is feeding well,' I say, at which point an obstetrician confers with the team and we're told we're free to leave.

The hospital staff have been wonderful. We've been constantly delighted by their attentiveness and kindness. We couldn't have asked for more and we feel ever proud of our NHS. But we're keen to settle Inigo into his new home, so there are fond farewells to the delivery team, a final sign-off – and then I face the most daunting task of all: working out how to fix our fiendishly complicated baby car seat into the car and manoeuvre our delicate newborn into it.

Inigo settled, I spot my flask of stone-cold tea – now four days old – and empty it before setting off at a speed so sedate we could have walked faster. At every junction I'm worried about accelerating or braking too quickly because of our precious cargo. Making my first journey with Inigo is more nerve-racking than taking my driving test.

We've called Alizée's mum to say we're on our way home, and Alizée has requested her favourite meal – calves' liver – for dinner as she hasn't been able to eat offal during her pregnancy.

Back home, our sense of time is blurred. We still feel that slightly hazy sense of disbelief. We introduce Inigo to his grandparents – Mum and Dad have joined us – and great-grandparents.

The dogs are intrigued by the new family member. I've got one of Inigo's muslins – I used it to wipe him down a little bit when he was first born – and the scent of him lingers. So I let the dogs smell it, and once Inigo has been cuddled by all the family, I introduce him to the dogs, one by one.

I settle him in my arms and the dogs come into the room individually. I tell them to sit, then I place Inigo's tiny hand in mine and allow them to sniff it.

Of all the dogs, Mabel is the most overwhelmed and excited. But we do not want to overdo it. Inigo is not even 24 hours old. It has been an eventful day, and he must rest.

Chapter Seventeen
In Loving Memory

——

The dogs take a keen interest in Inigo. Mabel is his self-appointed babysitter. If he cries and we're not in the room, she'll rush to tell us, going back and forth until we take notice. Isla likes to sleep under his pram; one of the dogs will guard his Moses basket or lie under his cot. I think they regard themselves as his surrogate parents.

When we go for a walk together, I swaddle him close to me and the dogs won't leave my side. They don't scamper ahead as they used to do, but stay close; they seem to know that if I have to call them I could wake the baby.

When one of them inadvertently gives him a wet kiss or when his hand touches their coat, he gives a little smile. I know he'll grow to love them.

We haven't been home long when we take him for his first outing.

Our local pub, The Old Boot, has been the focus of quite a few seminal moments in our family's lives, and now we take Inigo there.

We walk there with Alizée's mum and grandparents, and there are handshakes and hugs all round, some from people I've known all my life, as we wet the baby's head.

On the first weekend after his birth – it is hard to believe he is only two days old – my sisters and their children come to visit and we all have lunch together at Mum and Dad's. There are cries from the cousins of 'Was I ever that small?' and they take it in turns to cuddle Inigo in their laps.

They've worked out that there is a ten-year age gap between George and Inigo and they can't wait for him to be big enough to join in their adventures.

Mum and Dad are delighted by their new grandson, but Mum seems mildly incredulous that her little boy now has a son of his own. She laughs because she still thinks of me as her baby.

Sometimes I pinch myself too. It's crazy. I'm responsible for this precious new human life and I've stepped up into a new gear I didn't know existed. I'm not scared, though. I'm excited.

My sisters both have huge grins on their faces. It takes them back to the days when their firstborns were as tiny as their new nephew. 'Welcome to parenthood,' they say.

We are an affectionate and close-knit family and there are lots of hugs and laughter. Catherine and Pippa bring two big suitcases of hand-me-down clothes, so Inigo's cupboards are full of sweet little outfits that his cousins – even the girls – have worn.

We look at them and think, 'Aren't they enormous? It'll be months before he's wearing these.' We don't realise that he will grow so fast he'll fit them in a blink.

We're deluged with advice from my sisters, but we muddle through in our own way, sometimes getting things right, sometimes wrong.

During this first visit to my parents, I'm keen to show Inigo where Ella lies in the garden with Tilly and Mini. So we wrap him up snugly and I take him to her grave. It is a tender moment – and its poignancy still catches me – because I think back again to how far I have come.

My life was once so full of torment I felt suicidal. Only Ella gave me cause to keep living. She brought about this wonderful transition in me, from despair to hope. Today I have a wife and son I adore because of her. I never thought such a transformation could happen in my life – and it is all because of my Ella. I touch the picture of her in my pocket and blink away tears.

At home now I have a bronze cast of one of her paw pads. Pippa and Alizée managed to kidnap Ella during one family day and hold her still long enough to cast her paw in quick-setting plaster.

They gave it to me as a Christmas present a year after her passing and I keep it in our bedroom, another reminder of her.

Nick has given me a plum tree to plant in our orchard in her memory.

So she is here with me in all kinds of ways, tangible and spiritual. I feel her presence around me all the time: in her offspring; in a multitude of memories; in the person she has made me.

There will never be a time in my life when I do not think of her. And already she is a subliminal presence in Inigo's life.

There are moments in the still of the evening as I put him to bed when I talk to him about Ella. I make her the main character of the stories – some fictional, some true – that I tell him. It's never too soon, in my opinion, to introduce a baby to stories. Even before they are aware of their content, they are soothed by familiar voices. They watch the shapes your lips form as you articulate the words.

Ella is already there in Inigo's stories, among the first names he hears.

After I buried Ella, I sorted through her photos and put together an album of her life. I made one especially for Inigo, too, so she will be etched into his earliest memories. It sits on the bookshelf, leather-bound, for when he is older. There's a duplicate, too, with a wipe-clean cover, so he can leaf through with a child's sticky fingers as I talk to him about the pictures.

In it, the formative moments of Ella's life are charted. I look at the album now, tears blurring my eyes: Ella climbing her first mountain, the Old Man of Coniston in the Lakes; the same walk I made with Dad when I was little more than three years old.

Here is Ella swimming. There is the note she 'wrote' to Alizée and, for context, a photo taken outside the South Kensington Club so Inigo will know where Ella first introduced me to his mum.

On another page there is Ella, ears flying in the breeze, as she revels in her first cycle trip in the cargo carrier. Here she is, black bow tie round her neck, on the red carpet at the *GQ* awards. These are the moments that made up our lives together, immortalised in images as immutable and precious as my memories.

My aim is to talk to Inigo, when the time is right, about the struggles I had with my mental health, and how it was Ella who saw me through them. I want him to know, too, about the miracle of the animals that serve us and love us unconditionally. Guide dogs, assistance dogs, medical detection dogs. The dogs that help us through our darkest hours.

We think we are caring for them, but actually, in their own selfless way, they are the ones who are looking after us. They are the dogs who are saving our lives.

Acknowledgements

This book's origins go back to 2019 when I spoke publicly for the first time about my mental health. I was full of trepidation but my subsequent article in a national newspaper sparked such an outpouring of love and understanding that I wanted to expand the scope of my story and try to help others who were suffering similarly. So, I asked Frances Hardy to write this book with me, *Meet Ella: The Dog Who Saved My Life*, during which I shared the minutiae of my life as it unfolded – tears of sadness and joy, triumphs and tragedies, love and loss – and Frances helped translate my thoughts into prose.

But the book would not have come into being without literary agent Ruth Cairns, who spotted its potential appeal to anyone who has struggled with mental health problems; to dog lovers the world over; to everyone with an open heart and mind; and perhaps even to those interested in how our loving and close-knit family, the Middletons, tick.

But my utmost love and thanks go to my close family and friends (too many of the latter to name singly), who have stayed steadfastly beside me through everything.

ACKNOWLEDGEMENTS

I am thankful for the love of my wonderful parents, Michael and Carole; for my dear sisters, Catherine and Philippa, whose support has been unstinting; and for my brothers-in-law, William and James, for their kindness and understanding.

Above all, my heartfelt thanks to Alizée, the love of my life, whom I would never have met without Ella's intervention, and to our adored son, Inigo. The book is your legacy, Inigo. Through it, you will learn about Ella, and how she is the reason I am here to tell her story today.